The School on the Other Side of the River

The Educational Journey of Los Ricos de Abajo

Published by WILD RISING PRESS
Copyright ©2023 by Dianne Walta Hart and Carolyn Wells Simsarian

Editor: Judyth Hill
Cover and book design: Mary Meade
Credit for the front and back covers and interior photos goes to Billie Mercer and the many Los Ricos volunteers who contributed photos throughout the years.

Dianne Walta Hart and Carolyn Wells Simsarian—1st ed.
978-1-957468-12-9

The School on the Other Side of the River

The Educational Journey of Los Ricos de Abajo

Dianne Walta Hart

&

Carolyn Wells Simsarian

Wild Rising Press

EVERGREEN, COLORADO

This book is lovingly and gratefully dedicated to

Michael Chadwick

María de la Luz Jiménez Rodríguez (Lucha)

&

the community of Los Ricos de Abajo.

Contents

Part 4

Part 5

Part 6

We took baby steps,

grew where we saw the need,

pulled back when it didn't work,

and continued to show up

year after year.

Prologue

In the countryside near San Miguel de Allende, an NGO called Feed the Hungry San Miguel provides meals to students in dozens of elementary schools, including one in the small community of Los Ricos de Abajo. In addition, a group of volunteer English teachers shows up in Los Ricos every Wednesday during the winter months to teach the kindergarten students, the elementary through high school students, and the adults.

The stories recorded here take you from the very beginning of the English program through how it evolved and include the experiences of the students and the teachers; stories of the school director, Lucha, and one of the students, Yessenia.

Few programs like this have existed for as long as this one has: our longevity is a tribute to the teachers and the Los Ricos community. For those who may consider doing something similar, within this tale are lessons to be learned. For those who loved being part of it, there are stories ahead that will inspire you to rejoice, learn, and share.

The program began in 2006 and continues to this day. The idea originated with Michael Chadwick, the sponsor of the Los Ricos de Abajo kitchen, who wanted to do something more for the community.

San Miguel de Allende, Guanajuato, Mexico, a UNESCO World Heritage site, draws millions of visitors a year. Its arts scene, cultural festivals, restaurants, and hotels have earned first place designation in Conde Nast Traveler Readers' Choice Awards as the best in the category of Small Cities in the World.

Expats from the United States and Canada find the climate, the artistic culture, the cost of living, and the warmth of the Mexican people to their liking, making San Miguel a favored retirement destination. Increasingly affluent Mexicans are choosing to purchase second homes in San Miguel.

Yet, beyond the cobblestone streets of the central Jardín, the municipality of San Miguel has rural villages which have been described as a "ring of poverty." Statistics compiled through Data Mexico state that in 2020, 40.3% of the population was in moderate poverty. 3.76% live in extreme poverty. (Atención San Miguel, May 5, 2022)

Founded in 1984, Feed the Hungry San Miguel is committed to improving the health and well-being of children through school meals, nutrition programs, and community development. This organization serves meals in thirty-six schools, most in rural areas, every day during the school year. During the pandemic, Feed the Hungry expanded to provide food to entire families.

In 2005, Feed the Hungry opened a kitchen in Naciones Unidas, the elementary school in the rural community of Los Ricos de Abajo, and began feeding the children, as they had done in many other schools in the countryside around San Miguel de Allende.

Dianne Walta Hart has served on the Feed the Hungry Board and Advisory Council and has been active in the Los Ricos English Program since its inception, eventually serving as the Director of the Program.

Carolyn Wells Simsarian was introduced to Los Ricos in 2008 when she came to San Miguel de Allende for the month of March. She has been actively involved in the program since moving to San Miguel in 2010, developing curriculum and teaching in the 5-6 and 10-12 grades.

Feed the Hungry San Miguel provided the umbrella under which the teachers volunteered and without which the program and the educational growth of the students would not have been possible.

Find a Way In

~Carolyn Wells Simsarian

The history of Los Ricos
was not written
it was learned
from Lucha, Yessenia, Alejandro, Aidé
they tell their stories
of the river, the road, the village,
the school built by Benedictine monks

Perhaps in a cloistered library
after vespers
there is a brother
with a love of history
in addition to silence
comforted by legends
rare books long forgotten
perusing a manuscript

Accounts of hacienda lands
how they became ejido lands
every family given
a plot to cultivate
grow the corn, beans, and squash
plant, harvest and multiply
according to the cycles of moon and sun

Inevitable change
working for wages
to buy trucks
cellphones
internet and education
primaria, secundaria, prepa
so all may
follow a path.

After the past
the present
traveling together from
then to Now ...

Lucha and Yessenia
Alejandro and Fernando
record their stories
pass them down
for those who follow.

Dijo Mi Padre

—BY Yessenia Baltazar Ramírez

Dijo Mi Padre …
La medicina eres tú.
Son tus ancestros.
Es tu la tierra que te vio crecer.
Volver a tus orígenes siempre sana.
Pues es re-encontrarte contigo.
Recordar tu esencia.
Estás hecha de raíces.
De tierra.
Dijo Mi Padre …
Llevas en la sangre la valentía de tus ancestros te recuerdo que si caías de los
    caballos
te levantabas sin miedo y volvías a subir,
No te hacían falta zapatos, te recordamos
corriendo descalza por todos lados, feliz y cantando.
Subiendo a los árboles por más altos que fueran, jugando con serpientes
    vivas, desafiando las corrientes del río crecido.
Dijo Mi Padre …
A la chiflada lo que dices ¿Qué tienes miedo? ¿Quién te hizo dudar de ti?
Vuelve a tus orígenes, encuentra esa niña, esa niña salvaje la que no tenía
    miedo de nada ni de nadie, la que fue el dolor de cabeza de su madre
    por ser terca, testaruda y desobediente pero responsable con su vida
    a fin de cuentas, te aseguro que a pesar de sus diferencias hoy eres su
    orgullo. ¡Vuelve a ser tú!
Dijo Mi Padre …
Y ya no me encierres por qué no soy feliz,
Yo necesito estar en mi pueblo, yo soy cómo tú.
Yo nací para ser libre y si muero quiero morir en mi tierra y con mi botella
    en la mano.
Estas hecha de estrellas y has aprendido a brillar no dejes que nadie apague
    tu luz.
Dijo Mi Padre y comprendí tantas cosas …

So Said My Father

—Yessenia Baltazar Ramírez's Poem
Translated by Geoff Hargreaves

So said my father …
You are your own medicine,
And your ancestors are too.
This land that saw you grow up is you.
To go back to your roots is always healing,
For it means a re-encounter with yourself,
A remembering of your essence.
You are made from your roots,
From your land.
So said my father …
In your blood you carry the courage of your ancestors.
I remember when you used to fall off the horses,
You picked yourself up, without a qualm, and remounted.
You had no need of shoes. We recall you
Running barefoot everywhere, happy, singing.
Climbing trees, however high,
Playing with snakes, defying
The currents of the swollen river.
So said my father …
With this crazy talk you now speak,
What are you now afraid of?
Who made you doubt yourself?
Go back to your roots.
Find the little girl, the untamed little girl
Who was afraid of nothing,
Of nobody, such a headache for her mother,
With her stubbornness, willful and disobedient,
But, in the end, careful of her life.
I promise you that today, for all the differences,
She is a source of pride for you.
Go back to being her!
So said my father …

And don't lock me away just because I'm unhappy.
I need to be with my people. I'm like you.
I was born to live free, and if I die,
I want to meet death on my own soil, with a bottle in my hand.
You are composed of the stars and have learned to shine.
Let no one extinguish your light!
So said my father and so many things I understood.

Two important women in this book are:

María de la Luz Jiménez Rodríguez (Lucha), the school director, and Yessenia Baltazar Ramírez, a student.

Among the people you'll meet along the way are:

Aidé ~ Agustín ~ Alejandro ~ Alfredo ~ Bob Haas
Claudia ~ Estrella ~ Laura Jimena ~ Leticia ~ Luis Ángel
María José ~ María Maritza ~ Michael Chadwick ~ Rosa Elena
& the Los Ricos English Teachers

Contributing Organizations:

Feed the Hungry San Miguel
Patronato Pro Niños
Unitarian Universalist Fellowship of San Miguel de Allende
Mujeres en Cambio
San Miguel Writers' Conference and Literary Festival
Computadoras Pro Jóvenes
Lions Club
Rotary Club of South Whidbey Island (Washington)
Ezequiel Mojica and Apoyo de Gente Emprendedora
Caminos de Agua
Libros para Todos

Part 1

THE SCHOOL ON THE OTHER SIDE OF THE RIVER

CHAPTER 1

A Man with a Truck

Our story begins in 2004 when a man with a narrow-brimmed straw hat placed over his head so low that his eyes barely peeked out, pulled his battered truck to a stop on a dusty rural road in Central Mexico.

He rolled down the window on the passenger side and, in his piecemeal Spanish, asked a woman on the road if she wanted a ride. He had lived in Mexico long enough to know that he was breaking all sorts of rules, first by offering a ride to a woman he didn't know and then, even if he *did* know her, putting her in a situation where she'd be alone in a car with a man who wasn't a family member. He also knew that women would never—should never—accept rides from strangers.

Still, something about this short almost-middle-aged woman, looking a bit too professionally dressed for someone on a remote road, compelled him to stop. What the hell, he thought. The afternoon was as hot as Hades, and if she doesn't want a ride, she can always say no.

Even though this woman was alone on the road, she was not a country woman, and she said yes. Why not, she thought, it's been a long hot day. What's more, he didn't look like a tough guy and, she thought, smiling to herself, if he became a problem, she always had that machete in her big bag. She took this walk every day and dealt with packs of wild dogs, high river water, and an occasional drunk. She was a championship runner, too, faster than anyone who might think of chasing her. A gringo in a battered truck didn't scare her.

She got in.

In Spanish, he asked, "Where are you going?"

She kept her words to a minimum. "To the highway to catch the bus to San Miguel."

As the truck bumped down the road, he said, "Me, too." He waited a few seconds and added, "I can take you all the way. Too hot to stand out there and wait for the bus."

She nodded.

He added, "Where're you coming from?"

"Los Ricos," she said.

He had heard of the rancho, but in all the years he had been going to his nearby weekend home, he had never made that sharp turn to the left that would take him to it, past the monastery and across the Río Laja and up the hill. Funny name, Los Ricos de Abajo. The Rich from Below. Tiny spot. On a hill. Should be the Poor from Above.

"I teach school there. Naciones Unidas, an elementary school."

A teacher. It figures, he thought, as he glanced at her again, the way she's dressed and all. He asked her to tell him about the community he had never seen.

Her answers lengthened as she talked about the other two teachers, how they managed three classrooms full of students in grades one to six, the community's poverty, the odds against its residents, the price of being so far from the rest of the world, and how difficult it was to cross the river in the rainy season.

"You been there long?"

"Fifteen years. Since the school opened."

Fifteen years? He pushed his hat back a bit, dropped his sunglasses down on his nose, and surprised himself when he said, "I'd like to see the school, see that little rancho."

She laughed. Los Ricos didn't exactly have lots of visitors.

Then he added, continuing to sound incredulous, "Fifteen years you been walking to the school?"

"Yes."

They continued to talk as he drove her to San Miguel de Allende. She thought he had an odd accent and a sleepy way of talking. He appreciated her wonderfully precise Spanish, so good he could understand much of it.

He asked who built the school. He knew that no school district was taking care of these tiny ranchos other than hiring the teachers.

"People in the community. The priests in the monastery helped us with funds, too."

"After students finish that school, where do they go?"

"Those who continue—not even half—go to Atotonilco. It has a junior high school and a senior high school."

"Another long walk," he said.

"Everywhere is a long walk from Los Ricos de Abajo."

He had an idea and decided to mention it. Why not? The ride had been full of surprises. "There's a program I volunteer with. Feed the Hungry. They feed kids," he said, "lots of them. Maybe I can get them to do something with your school." He turned to look at her as if he were asking a question.

She smiled and nodded. She thought maybe something could happen. Just maybe. Foreigners had a way of getting things done. Sometimes. Always seemed to have so much money. But she also knew that they made a lot of promises they couldn't—or wouldn't—keep once they realized how difficult change was in Mexico. Even though she felt safe in the truck, who really knew what tipo de hombre this man was. Was he a man who kept his word? She didn't know.

As he slowed down in front of her house, he introduced himself. "Bob Haas."

"I'm Lucha," she answered. "Luz de la María Jiménez Rodríguez."

Months later, when both Bob and Lucha had forgotten each other's names but still remembered the promise, volunteers from Feed the Hungry San Miguel showed up at Lucha's school in Los Ricos de Abajo. The school was small for Feed the Hungry's guidelines, but when they saw it, they knew Bob Haas was right: difficult to reach for sure, desperately poor, and what's more, with a good school director.

They talked to Lucha about feeding the children. That's what we do, they said, and we've been doing it since 1984, and now we feed more than four thousand children every school day. We can feed yours.

Lucha nodded and thought to herself that it was a dream come true.

That's all it took for Feed the Hungry to clear the way with local officials and then arrange for Feed the Hungry funds donated by the Michael Chadwick family to be directed to the school.

The school consisted of a couple of buildings surrounded by a patio, a concrete court with basketball hoops (without nets) and a rudimentary dusty playground, all surrounded by a fence. Bob Haas rounded up his crew and a pal named Andy Swann and they designed a kitchen that would be attached to the main building and farther away, a latrine. The two showed up every Friday to check in with the workers and to dole out payroll and materials money.

In January 2005, Feed the Hungry began serving meals to the school children in Los Ricos de Abajo. Good to his word, Bob Haas had seen to it that Lucha got her kitchen.

"That's what happens when I offer rides to women," he'd laughingly add when he'd tell the story.

Lucha would laugh, too, when she'd talk about the hot long day when she broke her country's rules by getting into the truck of a funny-sounding stranger in a straw hat. She'd always add that now she knew what tipo de hombre he was.

This is their story. And ours.

CHAPTER 2

Remembering an English Father

The following year, 2006, Michael Chadwick and his family visited Mexico and saw in person the Feed the Hungry kitchen at Los Ricos de Abajo that their funds—along with Haas and Swann money—had financed, the cook who had been hired, the food that had been purchased, and the latrine that had been built.

After seeing the remote, poor but proud community, the Chadwicks began to wonder if they could do even more to improve the villagers' chances in the world. Feeding the children just didn't seem to be enough. Not in a place like Los Ricos de Abajo. What if they focused their efforts, stepped up the assistance, and then discovered what change could occur?

In response, Feed the Hungry collaborated with the Chadwicks and made the decision to teach English and start classes in 2006, a year after the kitchen had opened.

Michael Chadwick again visited the school and kitchen. He smiled happily through the kitchen tour, watched the students line up to receive their food, and knew he and his family had done a remarkable thing.

Then came the moment he climbed up the concrete steps to the tiny building that housed the fifth and sixth grades and entered the noisy classroom. Volunteer teachers had started teaching a few weeks earlier and found eager learners ready for them.

It was hard to miss Alejandro: fine featured, dark, thin, oozing energy. Raising his hand, leaping to show the teacher he understood, and wanting to take it all in. He was so short that when he wanted to be called on, he'd straddle the bottom rungs of his desk and the one in the aisle opposite him to be seen. Michael felt a rush of something he hadn't seen, a memory imagined over the years.

His father grew up in the English Midlands[11] where he was recognized by his teachers as bright and artistic, but he had to leave school after the third grade to work for his father in a small building business. As Michael continued to watch Alejandro, he wondered what his father, such an intelligent man, could have done with his life had he had more than three years of school.

Lucha had already talked with Alejandro's father about his son's being able to continue with school after the sixth grade. He was one of many children in the family and there was no money to pay for the schools, buy the books, or pay other expenses. Mexican public education came with costs that many families couldn't afford. Like his brothers before him, he'd work in the fields or learn to be a bricklayer's helper.

Well, Michael Chadwick thought, it's not going to happen to that little boy. As a result, Alejandro became the first recipient of the Chadwick Family Scholarship.

One day, as the volunteer English teachers finished teaching their classes for the year, they started talking about how other students would benefit from scholarships, not just Alejandro and not just those who showed early potential. One experienced teacher noted that you couldn't always tell in the sixth grade who was going to succeed. Some students simply took longer to start taking school seriously. Another said that there was so much we didn't know about these kids, their lives, their parents, the poverty beyond our imagination, and the culture so far from our understanding.

Right there, standing in the dusty parking area at the school, the teachers raised or pledged $1500 USD for scholarships. From that moment on, all students who finish the sixth grade at Naciones Unidas in Los Ricos have been offered scholarships to cover fees and expenses for further education.

Now all the students who graduate from the sixth grade go to the seventh grade in Atotonilco.

Bob and Lucha's kitchen, Michael Chadwick's sorrow about his father's loss, a little boy with lots of potential, and the energy and wisdom of volunteer teachers reached farther into the community than anyone had ever expected.

Born of these imaginings and inspiration, changes began.

---

[1] The Midlands are a part of England near the England-Wales border, Northern England, and Southern England. The Midlands were important in the Industrial Revolution of the 18th and 19th centuries. Wikipedia.

CHAPTER 3

Los Ricos de Abajo, Guanajuato, México:

A HISTORY

People have long been curious about the name Los Ricos de Abajo. Once you hear it, it stays with you. The Rich? From Below? But it's high on a hilltop. Some say it came from a family named Rico who lived there.

No one knows for sure.

Lucha's explanation of the rancho's origin is that many years ago people from nearby León, Guanajuato, came to the site where Los Ricos is now located with the idea of making shoes. After some time, those shoemakers offered similar work to the Otomí people of the surrounding communities. The story goes that when people were walking somewhere and met someone on the path, they would ask where the other person was heading. The answer would be "I am going to work with the rich, Los Ricos."

Eventually, the people who had been hired to make shoes stayed and built small houses for their families and so the community began to form.

Lucha doesn't know why the shoemakers left Los Ricos and returned to León, but when they did, some people had already decided to stay where they were, plant crops, and keep what the land gave them.

But the question continued to be: Where are you going? To Los Ricos. When it came time to give names to some communities in the municipality, they added Abajo. At the time, wealthy people already existed on the other side of San Miguel on the road that leads to Rodríguez, and that place was called Los Ricos de Arriba.

All cultures settled where there was water since it is essential for life, and Lucha says that's what the Otomí did: settle on the banks of the Río Laja to take advantage of the water for their crops.

To make everything more complex, after the Mexican Revolution, ejidos were created to grant lands to peasant communities such as Los Ricos. Later, as Mexico prepared to enter the North American Free Trade Agreement in 1991, President Carlos Salinas de Gortari declared the end of awarding ejidos and allowed existing ejidos to be rented or sold, ending land reform in Mexico.

CHAPTER 4

Dianne's Reflections on the Lucha Connection

At Michael Chadwick's request to do something more for the community of Los Ricos de Abajo, Feed the Hungry's first group of teachers went there two days a week in 2006 to teach English at Naciones Unidas, the elementary school.

One of the many challenges was that each of the three elementary school classrooms usually houses two class levels, e.g., first and second grades in one room, third and fourth in another, and then fifth and sixth. When enrollment drops a little, three levels end up in one classroom, making teaching more difficult. Fortunately, most of the time it is two levels per room.

Feed the Hungry had asked me to send requests in San Miguel's Civil List (an internet list that reaches thousands of residents) asking for English as a Second Language (ESL) teachers who could be substitutes for the small volunteer corps. Teaching there myself was not part of my plan. That is, if I had a plan.

Feed the Hungry had also requested that I write articles about their cooks for *Atención San Miguel*, San Miguel's bilingual newspaper. That task had taken me to Los Ricos a few times. I probably briefly met Lucha then, but I have no memory of her. I do remember interviewing the cooks in the Feed the Hungry kitchen, trying to figure out the history of what looked to me to be a nearly deserted village, and trying to absorb the shock of the desolate kindergarten building up the hill that had no door, no windowpanes, and no equipment.

One week in early 2007, Feed the Hungry asked me to substitute for the first- and second-grade teachers. My husband Tom and I had houseguests—a high school friend Bob and his wife, Lola—and we all said *yes*. Fortunately, Lola had been a grade-school teacher, so off we went.

Once in the classroom, only Lola wasn't bewildered in front of these rambunctious and out-of-control tiny kids. Just as I was reminding myself why I had never wanted to teach that age group, a little girl named Estrella stood on her seat. I admonished her and she got down. It happened again. The third time, she stood one level up, on top of her desk. Not on the seat but on top of her desk. Again, I told her in my most authoritarian voice to get down, a tone that worked with the teenagers I had previously taught, but Estrella's only reaction was a great big smile. The students thought it was hilarious. Lola had a better grip on the situation and went over to Estrella, picked her up, and popped her back in the seat.

So that's how you deal with tiny kids in a classroom, I thought.

About halfway through the class, the door opened and there was Lucha, much shorter than I and pointing up at me, beckoning for me to come with her. I wasn't quite sure who she was, but I figured it out when she said, "You must do something. Your volunteer English teacher in the fifth- and sixth-grade room is having trouble."

If that happened today, Lucha would march into the classroom even though a volunteer teacher was in it and her mere presence would silence everyone. But she was new to volunteer teachers and, for probably the only time in her life, unsure as to what the next step should be. I followed her short quick steps to the separate building that housed the older students. Along the way, however, I noticed students in the large playground who I later found out were the fifth and sixth graders from the classroom in question. To make it all worse, I saw one peeing on the concrete in front of everyone, letting us all know what he thought of the situation.

In the classroom, the teacher stood in front of the students, but the class was half-empty. The half to her right sat in their seats and looked at me with curiosity. (They had never seen me before nor I them.) To her left, the other half consisted of empty seats. I assumed they were the ones outside. As I know now, it was a rebellion because they didn't have their favorite English teacher Jackie and instead had a substitute. All I knew at that time, however, was that experiences from my past teaching kicked in, and after a short discussion, I asked them if they wanted to stay. *Yes,* they answered. I told them if they stayed, they had to behave. They agreed. I left, the room stayed quiet, and what Lucha did with those students on the outside patio, I have no idea. But I was grateful that my year as an assistant to the girls' vice principal in a South-Central Los Angeles junior high school was paying off. It was not the first time I walked into a teacher's classroom (one with older students, however) to attempt to find a solution to trouble.

The next year, I returned with the fifth- and sixth-grade teacher who had been absent that day, Jackie Donnelly. Our thought was that since Feed the Hungry and Michael Chadwick had made the decision for volunteers to teach at Los Ricos de Abajo, we were not going to be like so many do-good programs associated with NGOs who left when things became difficult. We would keep that promise, albeit in a different form. Instead of teaching two days a week, we would teach one; instead of trying to teach the whole school year, we would concentrate on the winter months when more volunteers would be available; and instead of looking for ESL teachers on the Civil List, I would ask for people who loved children.

That next winter, while the English teachers were teaching, Lucha and I would sit on the short stone wall around the patio. The advantage to her was that if she waited until we were done, she got a ride home, preferable to taking that long walk, the one where she had first met Bob Haas. The advantage to us was that I could sit with her, clipboard resting on my knees, and ask her the multiple questions we had about students and their backgrounds, about who built the school in the first place, about where to go to the bathroom (behind the bushes), why she had so few supplies, how in such a poor place some people had more money than others, why some people stole, why some always kept their word, why some never did, why families had a decades-long grudge against other ones in a Hatfield-McCoy way, and why she had such affection for this bewildering place on a hilltop that was also starting to enchant us. I would then pass on the information to the teachers.

Year after year. She kept us on track with the culture, what would be appropriate, and what wouldn't.

CHAPTER 5

The Río Laja

How's the river? The teachers asked each other at the beginning of every week in the winter teaching months. High? Can we get across? Anyone have any information? To the volunteer teachers, the river was a challenge.

The Upper Río Laja is bounded by mountain chains that surround a large plateau. The river, which flows from the Sierra de Guanajuato and through the cities of Dolores Hidalgo and San Miguel, is the area's primary river. It receives most of the rainfall not absorbed by the land and is the major source of water held in the Presa Allende. Below the dam, the river carries the water to the Río Lerma and onto Lake Chapala in the state of Jalisco.

Important as the river was, the questions remained. Had it flooded and taken out the road on one side? Both sides? Could someone go out there and check? The river bottom changed with each big rain, rocks shifted, and only a few locals with cars would know how to get across. Would our vehicles hit an unseen rock in the middle of the river? Would we have to park at the monastery and walk over that fragile little pedestrian bridge, three at a time, to cross the raging river? What about the teachers who had difficulty walking? Did we have a teacher with an SUV who would be willing to go from the monastery and back up to the school to transport them?

Then there was the private bridge. Maybe we could use that? The bridge was substantial, owned by a woman who needed it to access her own land, and we would use it for a good cause only once a week. I tried by posting a request on the closed entrance to the bridge. A few days later, a student's father called me. He worked on the woman's farm and, with heavy sadness in his voice, said that she would not, under any circumstances, let us cross.

As an experiment, we had Feed the Hungry take some of us in a small truck to Los Ricos via a long route over the back of the hill. Call us faint of heart, but that was our reaction to seeing paths to Los Ricos, not roads, marked only by plastic strings in trees. We'll stick to our traditional way, we said.

The old way meant we had to make decisions on the fly. One teacher, Lois Weiss, recalls a dramatic day: "All I remember is that the cars with standard undercarriages could not cross, and I was in one of them. I got out to alleviate the problem and mounted the fender of a Mexican's old SUV that was already filled with people. The driver—someone acquainted with the area—took me across at about two miles an hour."

Many students think of the river as a joy, especially when they were still in elementary school. As Alejandro said, "My friends and I played and swam—our adventures had no limits." Alfredo, now a university student, said that he remembers when the river had such clear water that you could see the fish going up and down with the current.

The rain that brought dread to the teachers was viewed differently by Jimena, another student, who said that what she most liked about having grown up in Los Ricos de Abajo was being able to enjoy "the customs—the nature, tranquility, history, religion—all that is part of it. Above all, I liked the river and arroyo in rainy weather."

Yessenia, one of Alejandro's contemporaries and playmates, loved the excitement. "I didn't get along well with my sisters and didn't like to play with them. Instead, I preferred to play with my brothers because they had more adrenaline. For example, we'd go to the river and swim against the current and on one occasion we came close to drowning! Usually, I went with my brothers, but one time my sisters accompanied us, and thanks to my uncle being there, they didn't drown. They never returned to the river to swim after that, but my brothers and I did. I loved to swim and wasn't afraid even when snakes curled around my feet."

Crossing the river could be a source of humor, as Leticia, a friend of Yessenia's, reports: "The water in the river was low, so I decided to cross it. The problem was that I didn't want to get my shoes wet, so I took them off. But as I got in the water and was busy with holding my bags aloft, I couldn't hold on to the shoes any longer and threw them to the other side. But what happened is that I threw the first one with enough momentum and it made it, but the second one didn't and floated away on the water. Hehehe. I died laughing."

As the years went on, people—especially those who had to go to work on the other side of the river—wearied of the challenge and began to look for solutions. Alfredo remembers having to take a back route to get out and go through other ranchos, and times they couldn't leave at all. The private bridge was out of the question, the pedestrian bridge had weakened again, and discussion began around a vado, best described as a giant cement culvert across the river. No guardrails, no lanes, but something that worked and was cheap. In times of gigantic floods, it would be of no use, but your average everyday large rainfall would be accommodated. The villagers talked with the county government, their local leaders, and began saving their required large share of funds and materials.

CHAPTER 6

Getting to Los Ricos One Day in March

This is a story of a typical day in our Los Ricos life.

We drive with a carful of volunteer teachers north from San Miguel on the road to Dolores Hidalgo. The road follows the terrain of gently rolling farmland, a fast-disappearing commodity as San Miguel grows outward. This road has the official tourist designation of Ruta del Vino: year-round brilliant sunshine and temperate climate support the cultivation of grapes and the development of Mexico's wine industry. During the time we've been visiting the school, we've also witnessed suburban expansion along the road, upscale gated communities which are often a source of employment for the people of Los Ricos, first as construction workers, then as gardeners and housemaids.

Along a bend in the highway, we pass signs announcing the turn off to La Gruta and Atotonilco. La Gruta is one of several similar day resorts built to take advantage of the thermal waters found throughout the area. These family resorts are popular with Mexican and international tourists.

Just past the Pemex Station, we pull into a left-turn lane. The road leads to the village of Atotonilco where the featured attraction is an eighteenth-century mission. The church's interior is richly decorated with frescoes depicting the arrival of the conquistadors and the conversion of the native people to Christianity. Christ is often referred to as El Conquistador—the conqueror of the soul. The church has a long history as a pilgrimage site for the predominantly Catholic Mexican faithful. Descendants of the conquered now have their own stalls to supply religious items, souvenirs, and snacks to the many visitors and pilgrims.

But before one gets to Atotonilco, a mile down the hard top, we turn right and quickly left onto a dirt road that takes us past a Benedictine Monastery, beautifully situated on a rise above open farmland. It was the monks of this monastery who, together with the people of the village, built the school at Los Ricos.

Continuing on the dirt road, we come to the Río Laja. On this day at the end of March, there are only about six inches of water in the river, and we can easily drive across the rocky bottom and up the other side. If the water is any higher, cars full of volunteer teachers often wait for a local truck or pick-up to show up and then follow it across the river to avoid the hidden boulders. Vehicles with a high clearance are needed to ford the river and the road. Lamentably, in making the trek, we've suffered some car casualties. There is also the problem of a face-off with the Coca Cola truck on the single-lane track.

The river is an essential feature of the landscape and in the life of Los Ricos. As Lucha notes, "All cultures settled where there was water." The ancestors of the inhabitants of Los Ricos settled here for all the reasons that their descendants have remained: water for household use, for crops, and for animals.

During the rainy season, the river can become a raging torrent cutting off the village from access to the outside world. Sometimes the Feed the Hungry volunteer bringing weekly supplies to the school lunch program cannot get through. Mothers often meet the volunteer and carry provisions across the footbridge. There was a season when the rains were so heavy during our program that we parked our cars at the monastery and used the footbridge. Now, on this day in March, we are about twenty minutes from the highway on our dirt road. The road is now narrower and more rutted.

We pass a small rusting shelter, a roof on two pipes which was once a bus stop. The bus arrives early in the morning and once in the evening; other than that, there is no bus service to Los Ricos and instead one must walk forty minutes out to the highway and catch a bus at the Pemex Station to Dolores Hidalgo to the north or San Miguel to the south.

Lucha did not have a car until the last few years of teaching at Los Ricos. She took the bus and walked the forty minutes to the school, armed with a stick to ward off aggressive stray dogs. There are no school buses. Students going to secundaria (junior high) or prepa (high school) in Atotonilco walk through the fields on worn paths, an hour each way.

During the dry season, the mesquite trees with their feathery leaves and the brush and dried grasses along the road are coated in fine talc-like dust. The dull tan of the dusty road envelops the foliage of the green leaves. As we continue along, we roll up the windows against clouds of choking dust. It is difficult to see the road ahead. We pass cornfields prepared for planting. Yessenia describes working with her family in her grandfather's fields. She remembers the stories he told her. How to plant "the three sisters"—beans, squash, and corn, together. These are the mainstays of the traditional diet. We pass a few houses built of adobe with corrugated metal roofs, grazing horses, a few cows, and a burro. Laundry is drying on bushes. Some houses have clotheslines, but no clothespins are necessary. In this arid climate, a week's laundry dries in an hour.

Now we are in the village with houses clustered together. The houses in the village are newer, made of concrete supports and crossbeams reinforced with rebar. Local brick fills in between. As a family's financial situation allows, the bricks and cement are stuccoed over and may be painted. A house on the left, newly painted with decorative columns, reflects a steady paycheck coming from adult children working in the United States.

On our right, in the center of the village, is the old church, with its surrounding stucco wall and bell tower. The church is open only for special occasions as there are not enough people in Los Ricos to support a priest.

To get to the school, we take a fork to the right. We are now climbing straight up a hard-packed, deeply rutted single-lane track. Our driver is going slowly, the car riding the ruts like a small boat riding waves in a storm. The passengers hang on as they pitch about in the back seat.

At last, we are at the top of the hill where the Escuela Primaria de Los Naciones Unidos commands pride of place in its spacious compound.

Lucha came as a teacher to Los Ricos and waited years before her appointment as director. From that moment forward, improvements began to happen. Top priority: a security fence around the school, which the government did approve.

We wait at the gate as students are sent running to the gate with the key to the padlock. They slide the bolt across and hold each side to admit the carbound volunteers who drive up past the paved multiuse basketball/soccer/fiesta court on the left and the forlorn swings and slide to the right. We park in front of a sidewalk that leads to the bathrooms. When they were built with funding from the Michael Chadwick family and other donors, these were the first flush toilets in the village. On Wednesdays, when we go out to tutor, students are coming from the bathrooms with buckets and mops, having readied them for our arrival.

What a welcome we receive in this remote, isolated village! Children, dressed in their navy-blue school uniforms, are all smiles on our arrival. "Hello." "How are you?" "My name is Estrella." "My name is Felipe." They practice their English greetings, taking our hands to lead us to the classrooms.

Part 2

THE PROGRAM & HOW IT GREW

Part 2

CHAPTER 7

Lessons: The Heart of the Program

L ike all aspects of the program, lesson planning and instruction have been
an evolutionary process. Grades one through six began with the volunteer teachers planning lessons. Where possible, the lead volunteer teacher
with teaching experience is paired with one or two assistant volunteers. At
first, there was a lot of volunteer turnover. We had an abundance during the
high tourist season. As interest in the program grew, we realized our program
and the students would benefit from more commitment and consistency. We
asked that volunteers commit to going out to Los Ricos and teaching for at
least eight of the ten or twelve weeks, making for a richer experience for both
students and volunteers. Students and teachers established all-important personal connections. Both groups looked forward to the start of the program
and seeing each other. As the years went by, we would get a shout-out from an
older student on the street in San Miguel. Such encounters were gratifying—
like old home week. Eventually, the high schoolers came to San Miguel every
Saturday for ongoing tutoring with volunteers Bob Bowers, Doug Lord, and
others at Doug's home.

While we went to Los Ricos to teach English, we soon learned that the
outcomes of the program were far larger and broader. Once the stone was
dropped in the pond, the ripples kept extending wider and wider. It was
not just about learning to communicate in another language. We must have
looked like strangers from another world when we first began the program.
Oldsters emerged from our SUVs in a cloud of dust. Students were shy; they
did not make eye contact. We had to put them at ease, establish trust. We
hoped they would learn more English, but we wanted them to have fun doing
it. We started classes with a song. There is no quicker warm-up. Big smiles
beamed out as every kid from kindergarten through sixth grade loved learn-

ing the words and movements to "Head, Shoulders, Knees, and Toes" and "The Hokey Pokey." Plenty of giggles when we put our "right hip in and shake it all about."

Name tags were essential. We learned their names; they learned ours. All classes taught greetings, which they were anxious to practice. "Hello, my name is Dulce Ramírez. What is yours? How are you today?" In those early days, the stress was on the English alphabet, the colors, the numbers starting with one through ten in the lower grades, familiar plants and animals, as well as foods and the objects commonly found in the classroom. As we came back year after year, we would review what was learned the year before and build on that. We found the students more at ease, comfortable to be around us and eager to learn. No more problem making eye contact.

The ripples in the pond kept expanding. Sixth grade had been the final year of schooling for the students of Los Ricos. Once the scholarship program was in place, the majority were choosing to go on to secundaria or junior school. Here again, access was key. What may appear to be a "lack of interest" to an outsider was actually due to the expense. While public education is free in Mexico, there were school fees, the cost of uniforms and lunches, expenses beyond what most families in Los Ricos could afford. Mujeres en Cambio, an NGO in San Miguel, provides becas (scholarships) for bright female students who cannot afford post-primary school, but competition is stiff. Some of our students qualified and received scholarships, but the average student, female and male, finds her/himself left behind.

Now, with access to scholarships, our students found themselves doing well when they went on to Atotonilco. We received reports that teachers were pleased and surprised by their head start in English. The students returned on Wednesdays to tell us that they learned more English from us because we were native speakers. Would we continue to offer English classes to them? Would we ever! So after the primary tutoring, followed by lunch, we were ready when they arrived, tired after having walked an hour on footpaths and a full day at their schools in Atotonilco.

CHAPTER 8

Expanding Worlds

In 2010, we contacted an architect, and with the help of private donors and Feed the Hungry, we cleared out the junk-filled extra classroom. A storage area called a bodega was built behind the school where school-district-owned wheelbarrows, bags of concrete, etc. could go. A small dining room (comedor) was built next to the kitchen. Here the children would eat in shifts and the space would double as a classroom for adults. Like many homes in the campo, the structure is simple, yet homey with warm brick walls and tables covered in brightly colored oilcloth. There is a sink in the corner for mandatory hand washing and a service window to the kitchen where students pick up their lunch trays. There were many benefits to this project. No longer would students have to eat lunches outside on a cold windy day in January. The freed-up extra classroom could now be turned into a Learning Center for computers and a library.

These felt like big plans at the time, with one step contingent on another. As each phase was completed the project fell into place. Lucha couldn't throw away the building paraphernalia because it belonged to the government, so it went into the new bodega. The cooks, students, the larger community, and we volunteers were happy to have a comedor in which to eat and teach. Donors contributed laptops for the Learning Center, and we put them in a safe to store the computers. A local internet provider promised to hook up the internet if we didn't tell any other NGOs or charities that they had done so. (They didn't want to be overwhelmed by non-paying customers). Deal. Today volunteers pay another provider for the service.

We eventually trained three Los Ricos high school students—Yessenia, Alejandro, and Maritza were among the first—in computer use and the internet with the promise of doubling their scholarships for the year if they taught other students. Three days a week, a few hours after school, only students allowed, and other essential rules. The word got out. Soon other students followed. According to Alejandro, "Working at the Learning Center taught me a lot about how to use a computer to do high school homework; great for all students."

Maritza adds, "Starting high school was a big change but not difficult. Yessenia and I were in charge of the Learning Center at Naciones Unidas and that changed my life by making it easier for me to do my schoolwork. Working there with Yessenia was a joy, the best afternoons of my life."

The teachers started donating books to the library and a grant allowed us to eventually buy shelves. At first, we optimistically brought English books, but it quickly became apparent that English wasn't going to work, so we switched to Spanish or bilingual books and hit the sweet spot. We wanted to teach them the joy of reading, no matter the language. Often reading isn't part of the leisure culture in Mexico in the same way as it is in many countries, so we knew the challenges. But to our surprise, it didn't come in the form of having to make the children read. They loved it, fought over books on horses, and adored anything with a princess. Fortunately for everyone, Jan Friedman and Pam Mosco, who had owned a children's bookstore, took over much of the initial planning and organization.

A schedule was made, and classroom teachers took the children to the library by grade. Eager to be the first in the door, students giggled and jostled each other in anticipation. Librarians were ready with volunteers to check in the books. Librarians assisted students in selecting books while others checked them out. Eventually, after experimenting with processes, the decision was made to have a volunteer go to a classroom, and a small number of students would follow him or her out in an orderly manner into the library.

Each student had a nylon mesh shopping bag to use as their library book bag. When they chose their library book, it went into the bag so they could bring it home and return it the next week. No one could choose a new book without returning the book from the previous week. So great was the desire to choose a new book that forgetting to return a book did not happen often. Once when a little guy forgot a book, tears were involved. The next week having returned the book and chosen a new one, he was all smiles. As the size of the collection grew, students were allowed to take home two books.

As students entered prepa, age-appropriate books were added to the collection. Harry Potter as well as several classics in translation became popular. Yessenia notes, "Thanks to the teachers, I read *Pride and Prejudice* by Jane Austen—she was a bit wild, just like me but in different times—and *To Kill a*

Mockingbird, and the book by Sonia Sotomayor, the first woman with Puerto Rican ancestry to become a judge in the United States. The world was opening up to the students of Los Ricos through the addition of the library and the pleasures of reading.

Libros para Todos, a San Miguel organization that encourages reading for children and young adults, brought Francisco Jiménez, author of the beloved classic *Cajas de Carton*, to Los Ricos de Abajo to read to the students. Students write of the thrill of collectively reading a book, hearing the author discuss the writing process, and receiving a personal copy of the book, signed by the author. This important exposure made the act of writing real to the students, further opening possibilities. Here was proof—actual real-life people write books. If this person can write a book, perhaps I too could someday write a book. The connection was developing, staying in school and getting an education, an important point made by Francisco Jiménez and other authors, could give a person more choices in life. Who knows? Perhaps someday a Los Ricos student will write a book. (Yessenia is well on her way!)

A year after Feed the Hungry started making meals for the students at Los Ricos, the San Miguel Writers' Conference and Literary Festival started. Every February authors, publishers, teachers, and readers arrive from the United States, Canada, Mexico, and Europe for a week-long celebration of panels, presentations, seminars, networking, and cultural events, as well as workshops for area high school students. The event takes place in a sprawling hotel with a series of conference rooms and a lobby full of famous people hobnobbing, worlds away from Los Ricos de Abajo. Could our students attend the conference, feel comfortable there and expand their own writing?

Thanks to one of our teachers, a local writer, Geoff Hargreaves, students were invited to attend the high-school workshops run by Rosi Zorilla and writer Duncan Tonatiuh. Los Ricos students were the only ones from a rural area, and they often felt the difference. However, they also got to know, albeit briefly, students from other schools. "Cute boys" was often the comment, or the same said about girls. The students attended conferences in rooms larger than anything previously imagined, famous writers gave them their books— Luis Villorio his *El libro salvaje* and Benito Taibo *Persona normal*—and encouraged them. Confidence seemed to be passed down from one year to another as the students began to strut through the lobby.

There was also the challenge to write better, and our students were up to it. Student Aidé won a laptop for having written the best essay. Others were singled out with compliments, and Luis Ángel says winning the creative writing contest in 2019 was the happiest time of his life. "I arrived a little late that day to the hotel, and they asked me if I was Luis Ángel and told me I had won first place with the story I wrote. They read my story in a classroom and then in front of many people from all over the world in a big conference room. I was too nervous to read it myself so one of the workshop teachers did it for me. Many people congratulated me, my parents were proud, and the truth was I felt very good." These supportive parents continue to be there for Luis Angel as he continues his studies. Volunteers felt tremendous pride that day, knowing all the planning and individual steps that contributed to building a school community where reading, writing, speaking, and literacy are valued. We were seeing concrete examples of student success.

There is a love of music everywhere in Mexico. We hear it in Centro wafting from restaurants, rooftops, passing cars and trucks, and parades. When a local music organization initiated a school-based program, they asked if they might come to Los Ricos. Again, Lucha welcomed the opportunity for her students. Pro Música supports concerts and opera, and, through its educational outreach programs, taught music at Los Ricos using indigenous instruments. After a concert featuring our students, they made a CD with the students' photos on the cover. When the husband of a volunteer teacher donated ukuleles, they made a CD with our students playing them.

One improvement led to another as the program grew. The physical addition of the comedor along with the building of the storage room, leading to the creation of the library, enhanced the educational program at Los Ricos. Other physical improvements would reap larger benefits. Through teacher Cathy Scherer, the Rotary Club of South Whidbey Island awarded the program a grant to buy desks and chairs for the teachers, school supplies, and file cabinets. Lucha said the classroom chair in her room was her first! The Unitarian Fellowship awarded us a grant to buy textbooks, and Computadoras Pro Jóvenes supplied the teachers with computers, again, their first ones ever.

Many of our teachers live in San Miguel full-time. Doug Lord offered the courtyard of his centrally located home for year-long Saturday English classes for the growing number of older students. This sounded like a terrific way to keep language learning alive during the months when we didn't go to Los Ricos and give support to students who were now entering universities. Bob Bowers, another full-time resident, signed on as a Saturday tutor.

As the program evolved, the Saturday teachers ended up being mentors as well as tutors. As so often happens, the best programs are in response to actual needs. We couldn't know the needs until they presented themselves. The flexibility of the program allowed for flexible responses and plans. Students knew that on Saturday around noon, Doug, Bob, and others would be there.

Students took the bus from Los Ricos to town, often attending a nearby computer class before class at Casa Lord. Classes were taught in small groups, laughter echoed throughout the courtyard, plans were made, emails sent, and problems solved. Mentoring fell naturally into place.

At times, Doug's home became the go-to place in a crisis. Yessenia writes of how important Doug's "safe house" was when her backpack along with her phone were stolen. Knowing she could go there and receive help was critical to her. Doug and Brianne's support allowed her to move beyond the incident and continue with her studies.

Finances for university students had to be administered and accounted for. We were fortunate to have Chris Peeters, Feed the Hungry's accountant, handle the finances at that end. Doug Lord, once again, stepped up. It all worked well since students knew he would be at home on Saturday morning. They could check in, bring their bills or receipts, and receive tuition funds. Doug and Chris would also arrange for the transfer of those funds for middle and high school students by having Lucha go to Doug's house, stash the money throughout her clothing, and go directly home. She would then go to students' homes to pass out the scholarships. She was able to do this before her retirement, receiving proof of school attendance and then handing over the pesos. After retirement, families would make appointments to go to her home.

One of the program's challenges is exposing students to the range of work/careers available to them. Students in Los Ricos are no strangers to work. Working in the fields planting and harvesting, tending animals the family raises, caring for younger siblings, preparing and cooking food, and doing building projects are familiar to them. The key was to expand opportunities through further training and education.

They started with entry-level jobs. Bob found work for some of the boys at a friend's restaurant, Don Lupe's Grill. Others have gotten jobs as hostesses, cooks, and waitstaff at restaurants and resorts that have sprung up along the highway in recent years. When asked about future goals, male students often responded that they want to be architects or, more precisely, builders, and many have been lured away from school at age fifteen to work in construction with an uncle or relative, starting out by carrying bricks. It's understandable that the offer of a job and one's own money is tempting.

The rapport among Doug, Bob, and the students grew through this year-round tutoring. Bob and Doug and other volunteers were invited and attended high school and university graduations. There were quinceañeras, fiestas, and weddings as well as the closing fiesta put on every year for the volunteers.

Meanwhile, we all had a good time taking in San Miguel offerings with students. Has anyone been to a movie in a theatre? No, the students said, propelling a group of us to take some high school students to the large theatre complex in a San Miguel mall. We got them there, gave them money for tickets for the matinee and a snack, and told them that we'd watch the same movie should they need us. We didn't want these teenagers to feel that they were being attended to by a group of gray-haired foreigners.

The theater was mainly empty, and our group of teachers sat midway up in the center. Then the students filed in. You could see them asking each other where to sit, and then they all proceeded to climb up the steps to sit right next to us. Guess being with us didn't look that embarrassing after all.

Hot-air balloons are often seen floating over San Miguel in the early dawn hours. Dipping low, one hears the loud whooshing sound, thus the name "the San Miguel Dragon." It's an experience for tourists and others to give one a different view of the expansive countryside. Would our students be up for the adventure, given the opportunity? Pilot Jay Kimball, Dianna Hutts Aston, and their crew drove up the challenging road with their balloon. Their goal was to tether the balloon to a hook under Kimball's truck and let it sail with students in the basket. Lucha took roll, reassured mothers as she took their permission slips, and kept order.

The gigantic balloon lay on the rocky hilltop. The balloon's bright colors—red, purple, green, gold, aqua, black, silver—contrasted with the dusty gray soccer field, its ends marked by two rusty goalposts and a smattering of mesquite trees. Finally, with a fan pushing cool air into the hot-air balloon, up it went, up, up, up, and then propelled by a blast of fire and fuel, it lifted off the ground. Poooof! The children jumped back and gasped, "Ahhhh," a sound echoed by their hovering mothers.

The children had stashed their backpacks under a mesquite tree. Some had said their prayers, and with Lucha's guidance, they lined up, sixth graders first. Out came a plastic box to help them climb into the basket at the bottom of the balloon, and ten to twelve students fit in. Then with a burst of flames, up they went, a big colorful balloon in the blue sky. Little hands could be seen waving from the basket, mothers could be heard calling to them, and the whole crowd—children, mothers, onlookers—watched with mouths open as this unlikely event took place in Los Ricos.

Later, two girls talked about how it felt. One said she had been nervous, but the other quickly added that she was not. They could see the countryside, they said, which they described as beautiful and commented on how tiny everyone looked. One could see her home; the other couldn't. They felt as if they were flying, their first time ever.

After making sure that all the children had gone, Lucha wondered if adults could go. Many previously nervous mothers and grandmothers crowded around the balloon, eager to have their chance, giggling more like schoolgirls than their own children and grandchildren had done. And Lucha? She managed to take two rides.[2] Yet another experience, an adventure, an opportunity. Now, when they hear the whoosh of the San Miguel Dragon, they can say, "I once went up in a hot-air balloon," a memory of a lifetime.

Under Lucha's direction, the students danced at a Feed the Hungry fundraising program at San Miguel's elegant Rosewood Hotel, an event the students and teachers still talk about. One student, Laura Jimena, recalls: "My favorite memory is when the volunteer English teachers arranged for us to dance at a Feed the Hungry event held at the Rosewood Hotel to raise funds for the school's comedor. We all wore white dresses; our hair and makeup were perfect. Our mothers were able to come to make sure everything went well. It was a beautiful event."

The program whose goals initially were to expose students in a rural village to English had evolved. No longer was it focused on one day a week for ten weeks with an hour of instruction. As volunteers became involved with the students, the school, the village, and its people, as needs were identified and plans were made and implemented, it was no longer simply about learning English vocabulary and phrases. Now it was about literacy—engaging students in reading, making books readily available, engaging them in writing and self-expression, and helping them gain experience and confidence in employment opportunities and themselves. It included exposing them to the arts and what was available in the larger San Miguel community. Students began to see the many rewards of further education as they successfully progressed through secundaria and prepa. Trust was built. Students knew that they could rely on us; we would be there for them. Volunteers were feeling the rewards of connecting to something larger than themselves, making a difference, to seeing positive change. It was hugely satisfying.

---

2 Adapted from an article for *Atención San Miguel* in 2009 by Dianne Walta Hart.

Part 3

VOICES OF THE DIRECTOR, STUDENTS &
ONE STUDENT IN PARTICULAR

CHAPTER 9

Maestra Lucha, the School Director

Through the years, my relationship with Lucha became personal, and we confided in each other as we searched for shade on the rock wall. My husband became her English tutor. I met her sons and her husband. We all shared her pride as her sons graduated from universities, two with advanced degrees in music whose concerts we attended. I wrote and published a story about her life, read it to an audience, and introduced her to everyone at the end.[3] She would occasionally come to some of our social gatherings at El Rinconcito, a San Miguel restaurant. When times were more difficult for her financially, she took a second teaching job in another town, which meant she had to walk to the Pemex station on the highway to catch the bus. But she still made time out of the school day to allow me to ask the most pertinent of questions. She eventually bought a Vocho (a VW bug), and then graduated to a used SUV, but again, she stayed to talk.

She was—and continues to be—our link to the community. I've lost track of the times I've said, "Let me check with Lucha." Today, years after her retirement, she makes recommendations as to which students are up for a certain responsibility, she distributes the scholarship funds to the seventh through twelfth graders after she collects the receipts that prove they're in school, and follows up when we encounter a situation that we cannot handle from afar.

She is our key to Los Ricos, our key to rural Mexico's culture, our key to the past, present, and future of the students. None of our success would have happened without her.

---

[3] "Thoroughly Modern Lucha," Dianne Walta Hart, *Solamente en San Miguel,* Volume II, 2010

IN HER OWN WORDS:
MARÍA DE LA LUZ JIMÉNEZ RODRÍGUEZ

I was born in the fall of 1960 in the same town where I now write these lines, San Miguel de Allende, Guanajuato. It goes without saying that San Miguel is a town full of magic and history, a beautiful place. They named me María de la Luz Jiménez and I was the sixth of twelve children from the marriage of Don Benjamín Jiménez Dorantes and Doña Josefina Rodríguez Godínez.

The name María de la Luz stayed with me for a while. When I was born, I was so small that my cradle was a shoebox. That's where I fit. Since they thought I wouldn't survive, they entrusted me to the Virgin de la Luz. As I grew up, I was called Lucita, and the name Lucha began when I started my studies to become a teacher. They said, "You honor your name because you fight to get everything you need for yourself and for others." So Lucha it is.

My childhood with my parents passed calmly and happily until one winter night during the Christmas posadas that represent the nine-day journey to Bethlehem. I was about to turn six years old. A man who was sitting in a doorway grabbed me and put a handkerchief over my mouth. I don't know what the handkerchief contained, but I dozed off and didn't wake up until I heard a door opening in a building where he had taken me. I told the man that my mother was going to come. He threw me on the floor, but I quickly got up and started running. This all took place in the outskirts of San Miguel, and although the man followed me, even at my young age, I ran faster than he.

By the time I reached the central streets of San Miguel, the town was alarmed, and my mother, older brothers, and others were looking for me. When I saw a large group of people, I shouted that a man wants to kidnap me. The people and two policemen ran after him. Upon seeing that, the man fled until he reached a bridge, the Puente de Guanajuato, and then he jumped into the arroyo and ran away. To this day, I have not forgotten this, but I can say that I overcame it, with simple Mexican courage, or as we say in Mexico, al puro valor mexicano.

Maybe that's made me like the sport of running so much. In high school, I stood out for being a sprinter and competed in various parts of the state—but not at the national level because my father wouldn't give his permission for me to participate out of state. I also ran in foot races organized by the county. Whenever I competed, I won prizes, but the best for me was in 1975 when they began El Día de la Mujer and I won first place.

My life continued with my parents, living in a humble but happy way. I went to elementary school, then secundaria, but that's when the charm ended.

My father, whom I loved very much, told me, "Well, now, daughter, I've supported you until now but if you want to continue studying, you have to do it on your own." Then he continued, "You were the first of your siblings to want to go to secundaria, but now the others are asking to do what you did, and I can't afford it."

I had to look for work and study at the same time, but it was difficult. I had made up my mind to be a teacher when I was in the sixth grade, so I looked for a way to go to a teaching school where I could also work and pay for my expenses.

To do that, I worked in a carpet workshop, in a sweater workshop, in a tortilla shop, in a hotel, in a tire distributor, and finally, I joined a system called CONAFE (Consejo Nacional de Fomento Educativo/National Council for Educational Development) that consists of supporting young people to work and study. During the week from Monday to Friday, I taught in a nearby community named Oaxaca (near the rancho called Cruz de Palmar) and on weekends I studied in the city of Guanajuato. That's how I was able to work and study and fulfill my dream of being a teacher.

My education continued, and even after I was teaching, married, and with children, I studied for a Bachelor of Education and then in 2000, I received a master's degree in educational sociology.

But now back to when I was finishing the normal (teaching) school, that's when I got married and Fernando, my oldest son, was born. At that time, there were few openings, and it was difficult to get a job as a teacher, so I started a grocery store in my home, which turned out well, and I did it for nine years. During that period, my second son, Guillermo, was born. About then, a teacher I knew who taught at Naciones Unidas in Los Ricos offered me the opportunity to teach there. I turned it down because I was comfortable with my store. He offered me the position two more times, and finally, I decided to do it. On March 1st, 1990, I arrived at the Naciones Unidas school.

I was enthusiastic to do my job in the best way possible, and I ended up falling in love with my work, the school, and the community, so much so that I started teaching there in 1990 when I was 30 and finished 30 years later.

When I arrived at the Los Ricos de Abajo school, it seemed forgotten by the educational and government authorities and was rarely, if ever, visited during the school year. The school did not have electricity, it did not have a fence or wall around it, it did not have toilets, which were, one could say, necessities for students. Although Naciones Unidas was a marginalized school in terms of support, above all it seemed to lack the desire to progress.

The teaching staff was not committed to their work and the person who served as the director expressed, "It is not necessary for students to learn great things since in the future they will only count their livestock." In effect, that's what the parents thought, too; all they expected was that their children would learn to read a little and then the parents would take them out of school to help them with agricultural activities.

The teachers worked without enthusiasm as if their only duty was to faithfully complete their five-hour schedule. Sometimes a teacher, who was explaining something by writing on the blackboard, wouldn't even notice that everyone had left. There were no students left in the classroom. In truth, there are endless anecdotes like that.

Naciones Unidas was a tridocente, which meant it had three teachers, but only male teachers had taught there. As a result, when there were meetings of parents, it was mostly men who attended. In 1995, when I became director—you would say principal—mothers started to show up, one after another, soon only women attended the meetings. I'd like to think that the women felt good that the director was a woman, or perhaps, the men thought their wives would understand me better than they did!

Many things made the community appear marginalized. Two obstacles made it difficult to get there. The first, the deeply rutted road, was man-made. Most such roads in Mexico are maintained by men with shovels, but there was neither the time, money nor materials to do so. The second obstacle was the river, a natural barrier that during the rainy season seemed determined to let no one cross. But the fact was, we teachers had to cross the river to get to the school and do our job. One year when the Río Laja was full of water, the villagers took an old suspension bridge used for pedestrians and started to repair it. The repairs took almost two years to complete. In the meantime, we had to swim or ride on mule carts across the river. We even floated to the other side in tubs, like bathtubs but made of strong plastic. Men and women who knew how to swim would put a tub in the river and then the people who had to go to work or to school—six at a time—would be transported back and forth across the river.

When they finally managed to put in place the suspension bridge, it was just the ropes of the bridge, and we had to learn to cross the river on those ropes if we did not want to get all wet. (I speak in the plural because there were students from other communities, another teacher who was from San Miguel de Allende, and others from the community who had to use the bridge.)

Most of the students lacked clothes, shoes, toys, and school supplies; the list goes on. People seemed resigned to what appeared to be their lot in life. To me, the most worrying thing was the lack of a good diet. When students had to stand in a formation during opening morning exercises, participate in civic acts, or conduct some other activity, some fainted, even when they stood in the shade. For me, that was a big challenge.

I wanted to find a way to instill in the community the desire to have a better life. I wanted to inspire them to set goals and help them see that through education, study, and work, change was possible. However, I was under the orders of a director who thought differently.

Time passed and with it came changes. I wanted people to aspire for something better for their children than just studying in primary school. The problem was that to continue their studies in junior or senior high school, the students had to go to the neighboring community of Atotonilco. The road was impassable, there were no cars in Los Ricos and there was no chance of buying them. It was difficult to encourage students to continue going to school when they couldn't see opportunities. But gradually people started working in San Miguel, and thus the community began to change.

In 1993 my third son, Eduardo, was born. My children got to know the school because when they were little, I took them with me even though the trip was a five-kilometer walk from the bus stop to the school and the same five kilometers to return. When I started in 1990, Guillermo was three and I carried him to school, and after Eduardo was born, I sometimes did the same with him. Fernando went on occasion, too, but I didn't have to carry him. This happened only when there was no one to take care of them and it was usually one child at a time. All three, however, accompanied me for festivals, like El Día del Niño and El 10 de Mayo, Mexico's Mother's Day.

In 1995, I was appointed director of the school and from that moment on I began to look for help and to point out to our educational and government authorities that there was a small school on the other side of the river that also needed to be visited. Little by little that's what happened. First, they put a cyclone fence around the school. Later, I was able to get a multipurpose court and some other things, like the electricity and water system improvements.

What worried me the most were the basic needs of my students. There were times when they stopped attending due to lack of shoes, lack of pants or their most essential tools, a pencil, or a notebook, etc., but above all, they needed food. In addition to more food, it would also be necessary to specify the importance of a good diet so that the children would perform better. I needed to look for strategies to achieve this ... I didn't know if I could bring in specialists who would talk to the parents about what a balanced diet is like without spending a lot of money. There were also those obstacles of distance and access to the community. Time passed.

I believe God's timing is perfect. One day in the year 2004, I found an angel on the road who asked me if I wanted a ride to San Miguel. During the trip, we talked about my work and about the good works that Feed the Hungry does, and that angel, Bob Haas, told me that God sent him to help me in my work. After promising that he would visit me at the school, he dropped me off in San Miguel. A few months passed, and I thought he had forgotten about me and the needs of my school, but one day, OH! A BIG SURPRSE, Feed the Hungry came to the school. With it came many good things that would create a radical change in the school and students as well as in the community for which we'll always be grateful. Bob Haas was the link with the altruistic organization. It began with the construction of a kitchen and then Feed the Hungry began by giving breakfast to the students.

The kitchen was sponsored by an American man, Michael Chadwick, and this changed Los Ricos de Abajo. A nutritionist and a chef participated and taught the mothers how important good nutrition was to the growth and development of children. The program measured each student's height and weight. If a child wasn't developing appropriately, mothers were given recommendations as to what to do to improve their child's diet. The children also received talks about nutrition and hygiene. You could see the change in school achievement, in discipline, and in the students' faces. Mr. Chadwick saw that the kindergarten up the hill had no doors and no windowpanes; he took care of that, too, making sure the doors and windows were installed and the building was habitable.

Then in 2005, at Mr. Chadwick's request, a group of foreigners organized by Feed the Hungry came to join the school's team of teachers and offered to help teach English from January 2006 until the Easter vacation. They brought with them many improvements—a dining room was constructed, a storage room, and flush toilets.

After the volunteers taught the elementary school students, they taught the adults and older students. They also brought computers to the school and the internet, all this to a community that not long ago was said to be marginalized. Many benefits came to the school and its students—the young people of the community were able to continue their studies with scholarships to secundaria and preparatoria.

When they arrive every January, it is a pleasure for all of us to have them with us because we—the children, the teachers, and the community—have become accustomed to their presence and have come to feel great affection and gratitude.

They came to stay, and it is an honor and a pleasure to have them every winter.

Everyone in the community has received support from this group of volunteer teachers since not only were young people able to go to junior and senior high school, but eventually to university. Some have already finished and are professionals.

I stayed at Naciones Unidas for thirty years. At the end of my career as an employee of the SEG (Secretaria de Educación Guanajuato/Office of Guanajuato Education), I could leave with the satisfaction of having left a mark on the community of Los Ricos de Abajo.

My children are Luis Fernando who is a Licenciado in Graphic Design, José Guillermo who studied music and was a military musician in the army's Twelfth Military Region, and José Eduardo who is about to finish his music career at the University de Guanajuato. And now I have my little grandson Guillermo, born in late summer 2018.4

Guillermo, who died soon after his son was born, was the second of my three children, an exemplary, kind, sociable, loving son. He studied in San Miguel de Allende from preschool through high school. Afterward, he went to León where he studied engineering for six semesters, but he quit because his true passion was music. When he returned from León, he worked for a year for Chrysler cars in San Miguel, and then decided to study music and English at the Universidad de Guanajuato. He was always a good student and almost every semester he was awarded and recognized as outstanding.

Then there was a call by the Secretary of National Defense to form the army's first wind band (woodwind, brass, and percussion instruments) in the area that includes Querétaro, Guanajuato, and Michoacán. Both Guillermo and Eduardo tried out, and with so much pride I can say that both were accepted. However, when it came time to sign the contract, Eduardo decided against being part of the army band and only Guillermo stayed. He continued studying at the university because he still had not finished his eight levels of English. Within the band, he developed as a professional musician. He received many awards and the most important was when his group won first place at the national level in the wind band contest. For a time, his band belonged to what in Mexico is called Monumental Banda del Ejército Militar (Army's Monumental Band) which participates in major military and social events. He excelled in the band, too, and won a competition for a porra, like a symbolic chant that represents the band. Even today when they play, they announce that it was composed by Guillermo.

Then came the terrible day in September 2018. I tried to communicate with Guillermo without getting an answer, and I began to worry because I talk with my children twice every day—once in the morning and then also at night. But that day he didn't answer me; I called again and again and once more at night and no answer. Finally, at 11:00 p.m. I received a call from Irapuato that they had taken him to the Hospital Central Militar (Central Military Hospital) in Mexico City. I immediately got in the car with my son Fernando and his father, and we headed to Mexico, arriving around 4:00 a.m. My son was already gravely sick, even without a diagnosis, but everything pointed to a frightening disease: leukemia.

The torment began. His brothers, his father, and I took charge of finding blood donors, and then Fernando and Eduardo transported the people from San Miguel to the Mexico City hospital and afterwards returned them to San Miguel. At the same time, my husband was attentive to those who needed to care for my son. I took care of Guillermo and suffered the helplessness of not being able to do anything.

Thus, the days passed, as did the month. I do not remember having slept one night, never going to bed all night in a bed, only sitting or standing, and always paying attention to what my son needed. But no more could be done until the day of October 16th, after spending two days in intensive care, my son left, never to return. He was a great man, a great musician, and I will carry him in my heart until my end.

I retired on the first day of October 2018 with great sadness, of losing one of my children, but I was also left with a beautiful blessing of a little grandson. I was always a happy and enthusiastic person, giving my heart, my time, and my life in the service of that school and community, not just educating with the blackboard but with my heart. But, as I've told you before, my children are the reason for my life, the motor that drives me, and now with this pain ... I don't know what will happen since the day my son's heart stopped beating, mine began to die ...

CHAPTER 10

Los Ricos Students in Their Own Words

ALEJANDRO

I don't know how much schooling my parents had, but I do know they didn't have more than elementary school. My father was a farmer in Los Ricos de Abajo and my mother was a housewife. My childhood was the best without luxuries or much in the way of material things, but I was one of the happiest people and to this day I do not regret anything in my childhood.

What I liked the most about growing up in Los Ricos de Abajo is that more than once I had to fight to achieve something, no matter how insignificant it was, I would gladly go back and live that life again. My roots are in Los Ricos, and it is something that I will never forget, something that stays deep within me. I liked doing something different every day, and so my friends and I played and swam—our adventures had no limits.

The friends I still have there are few, but my happiest memories are the years in Naciones Unidas, surrounded by all my classmates and teachers, excellent educators who today have my respect. I would not really change anything since what I experienced at Naciones Unidas was my greatest happiness. Even today, I remember my time with my teachers and my classmates, and when I talk with some of my friends from elementary school, we talk about old times, and we laugh at what we went through. It is good to go back to the past from time to time.

The teaching program came to Los Ricos for the first time when I was in my sixth year. I remember it perfectly; I have always been a person open to anything and the teachers who arrived on that occasion motivated me to continue studying. At first, they seemed strange to me, but with the passage of time, I liked them. They were great people, all charismatic. The classes were the basis of our education because they strengthened our vocabulary. One of the lessons that I still have engraved in my memory is to ask permission, greet, and say goodbye, simple things that as people reflect who we are and how we are.

Leaving elementary school and entering secundaria was a radical change, something totally new for me, but I was so enthusiastic that it didn't bother me. I had excellent teachers, and my favorite subjects were math, biology, English, and Spanish. I was fascinated by everything related to biology and, of course, English because we studied it in elementary school with the volunteer teachers. I was never a student who had grades of ten, but much of what I saw in books I now apply in my life. Especially the practical matters more than the theoretical, what I learned empirically. The subject most difficult for me was history; it's not that I didn't like it, but that I never fully understood it. If I could speak another language, it would be English, but I would like to speak Chinese or Japanese, too.

In high school at SABES (Sistema Avanzado de Bachillerato y Educación Superior) in Atotonilco, I liked all the subjects. I learned to change my way of studying: it was more methodical, I understood more what I was reading and doing, and I focused more. There were days when I had long homework assignments, and somehow, I did them. That stage in high school was pleasant. After school, I would play soccer with my friends. On Saturdays and Sundays, I worked at the Escondido Spa or in a blacksmith's shop with my cousin.

I like reading, but I have never finished reading a book. I am a person who reads one or ten pages and then sees another book or something else to read. I'm not much for watching or playing sports, but I like volleyball and soccer. But I would like to clarify I don't like American football. I am not delicate, but I find it rough.

I had only one ambition from elementary to high school which was to be a nurse or a doctor. After that, my opinion changed, and I decided to be a lawyer. What caught my attention was criminology, and I started Centro de Estudios Superiores Allende. I would have liked to have been a perito (detective). Criminology is everything related to the human being in matters of autopsies and necropsies, and I find all aspects of that career interesting. Unfortunately, I could not achieve my goal. I left after a year and a half.

I was one of the students the teachers helped the most—all the time and without any conditions. I was also one of the people who gave up along the way. But apart from all that, I thank with my heart in hand the whole group of volunteer teachers of Feed the Hungry. The scholarship that was awarded to me was a great help because I was one of the people with few resources and the scholarship helped pay for a large part of my studies including materials needed for work in the classroom.

If I had the opportunity to give my own family, my wife and children, something, it would be to always be united. Thank God, my father taught us to work, to use our own hands. My mother, without a doubt, is a great woman. Both instilled in us the necessary values that allowed us to differentiate good from evil. Materially we always needed money. We did not have the comforts that many others had, but the union is what lasts in my family. I hope it will continue to be so for many more years.

AIDÉ

I was born in San Miguel de Allende in 1997, but I grew up in Los Ricos de Abajo, a small village where I went to elementary school. That's where I learned about Feed the Hungry when they opened a kitchen and began serving lunches at our school. I always enjoyed the meals. Not long after the lunch program began, volunteer teachers arrived and began to teach English.

My childhood was memorable because we all knew each other in the community. My childhood in Los Ricos was a beautiful time. I was always with my family; I liked to play soccer, study, and learn English.

I also remember that my biggest dream was to be a cosmetologist and do make-up and hair. For junior and senior high, I went to Atotonilco where I met many new people, but I never imagined continuing to study, yet I was someone who longed for a different future. The time came when I had to decide what the future would bring. The English teachers and my mother encouraged me to continue studying. My mother wanted me to have a better future.

I entered the Universidad de León located in San Miguel de Allende. Within the university, I met many people who made me want to improve myself and that inspired me to continue studying. At the university, I met my best friend Alondra, a great person who made me believe in myself and in my intelligence, and Luis Ángel González, who with his love and patience, made every day memorable, made me believe that everything was possible, and always reminded me of a person I could be. These two friends helped me develop my character as a human being.

I've always had good friends, even in Los Ricos, and I love returning and walking the streets and greeting all the people I know—it makes me realize how good my time there was.

ROSA ELENA

My years in Los Ricos were great. Every afternoon I played outdoors in the strong wind with my cousins on the soccer field. I remember the incredible sunsets that were drifting behind the field while playing at the house of Yessenia, who was one of my best friends. We played soccer or played with slightly worn toys that were our gifts on Three Kings Day. Happy as always. I remember that in my house there were beans for us to eat outside along with soup, rice, or potatoes with red chili, and when my mother was paid on Saturdays, we had some chicken.

Apparently, everything could not continue being perfect since my most difficult moments were when I was diagnosed with lupus. If I could change anything, I would change that. I could no longer walk because it gave me extreme pain in my feet to the point that I cried a lot. I could no longer play soccer; I couldn't go to school; I couldn't move. I had to use sunscreen all the time, which was expensive, and my mom had to stop buying other things to afford it. I had to wear a cap or hat because the sun damaged me. Other children used to ridicule me and call me names—what we now call bullying. I think that made me stronger, as did going to all the medical consultations in León.

My mother never gave up and fought for me to be well. It took four years until one day the doctor said it was difficult to explain: the tests showed that I no longer had the disease. We were all surprised because lupus has no cure. My mother says that miracles exist and that was one of them. Thank God.

I felt fortunate when the volunteer English teachers showed up to teach us their language. At the beginning, it made me a little anxious to talk to people as big as Americans, since being in a rural community, I never imagined that we would have American teachers. It was like a dream. A dream I remember, thanks to the English classes. When I went on to secundaria, I was one of the outstanding ones in that subject and surprised my teachers by knowing all the body parts and could even sing about them.

When we graduated from the sixth grade at Naciones Unidas, they put on a concert, and we wore caps and gowns. It was fantastic with a huge chocolate cake, my favorite flavor.

Some of the teachers are still in my mind: Jackie who always told me that I was tall like her, Doug who has always been such a nice and good person with a big smile, Dianne who is one of the best people in the world (and thanks to her brother, Doug Walta, I was able to continue my university studies). Señor Bob and Geoff also helped me a lot, as well as being so much fun. There is also a special person who taught me her French language: Gigi, I remember all her classes and her laughter when I didn't pronounce something well. Thank you to everyone for the scholarships that allowed me to study in secundaria, through high school, and then university.

I did my first hotel internship in Cancún and then Nancy Morrin Zimmerman and her husband, Bob, helped me fulfill my dream by helping me with the best experience of my professional life: another hotel internship, but this one in a hotel in Costa Rica. All my life I will be grateful for such a great gift and the many opportunities. I will never forget them.

Even though everything is a sacrifice and difficult right now with Covid, I know it's better to study and thus be able to find employment or to generate ideas, your own ideas for the future. The best thing I have done in my life was study, but I would never have accomplished anything without the English teachers! Now I have a small daughter and I want the best for her, so we will encourage her studies.

MARÍA MARITZA

In my youth, I was happiest when we went to our English classes, especially the afternoon when they took a group of us to the movies at the Luciérnaga Mall. I was always the saddest when my father went to the United States.

My most difficult time was overcoming being raped. I'm sorry to have to say it so directly, but there is no other way to put it because I want to be honest with the teachers who gave me so much.

I have no desire to change or forget everything because everything that happened to me and every decision I made helped get me to the place I am now. Overcoming adversities and obstacles has made me strong.

Even if I did not finish college (I stopped during my first year), I did finish high school. At one point in my life, I thought I wouldn't even be able to attend either one. When the English classes began in Los Ricos, I was no longer in secundaria, because I had to stop after finishing the ninth grade due to a lack of resources. When I learned that the teachers also awarded scholarships to students who graduated from Naciones Unidas even before they arrived, I went to find out if I was eligible. I was thrilled to learn I could continue my studies, thanks to the English Program.

When I started English classes, it allowed me to do even better in high school. We attended the volunteers' classes every Wednesday—all good teachers, patient, some old, others not, and sometimes it took us a while to catch on. I also learned that even though every day the world suffers from crime and evil exists, there are still good people who help selflessly and with huge hearts. That motivates me to be a better person every day.

I finished high school, and I was in the first year of university when my little Leila was on her way, and it was a high-risk pregnancy. I live now in unión libre[4] with the father of my daughter and even though we're not married, I call him my husband because we've been together for several years.

I have thought about doing an English course online so that in five years I can be a bilingual woman. In ten years? I would like to study to allow me to get a good job where they pay me more and then save to start a business in the small community of Las Cañas where I live. I have thought of a pastry shop or a small fonda/restaurant.

If I could tell myself or someone else in their last year of high school about the future, I would say that good things and bad things will be ahead, but nothing that you cannot overcome and that you can't face with courage. Afterward, something good will come. After every storm always comes a rainbow.

LUIS ÁNGEL

My favorite memory from Naciones Unidas elementary school was when they held a poetry contest, and I participated. So did other people, but the difference was that the whole school supported me. I did not expect that, because I hadn't talked to all the students in the school, but I was happy when I won first place. After that event, I recited that poem again, but now in front of more people and on a large stage, with important people listening to me. I won again, but now third place; it was at the municipal level with students from all over the county.

All my Naciones Unidas teachers were good for my academic development, some in one area, others in another. The truth is that every time I changed teachers, I felt lucky because each teacher had a way of teaching, expressing herself or himself, explaining that all they wanted was to help the students and with me they succeeded. They helped me a lot, and now I want to go far in life and make these teachers feel proud of me. I want them to know that without their help, I would not be where I am now.

My favorite class in junior high was chemistry, and my least favorite was math because I hardly understood the teachers. In high school, my favorites were chemistry and biology, because I liked experimenting in the laboratory.

And I also had a teacher who encouraged me to participate in a poetry ompetition, guided my vocational search, and has given me many writing tips, which I have put into practice.

---

[4] A common-law marriage.

If I could go to another country, I'd go to Paris, France, not to visit the Eiffel Tower but to go to the Museo del Hombre (Musée de l'Homme), an anthropological museum there. I'm interested in French language, culture, and art. I've been studying English and am a little advanced—I feel comfortable speaking it and I like it—so I'd like to study French, especially if I travel there.

I'd like to be a veterinarian—I like biology, chemistry, animals, and medicine—and it comes with many professional opportunities and a good salary. I'd like to be a veterinarian or a Licenciado in Literature. In five years, I will have finished university and working in my profession. In ten years, I see myself taking care of many animals, having my own house, a car, and being more responsible and intelligent. I hope to write a book before those ten years are up. I see myself being even happier.

I think I haven't had any hard times, just good times.

CLAUDIA

I really like Los Ricos because there I can enjoy nature. Growing up there was wonderful, too; I had fun with my friends and cousins, and I have to say the most beautiful time of my life was my childhood. The most difficult time was leaving Naciones Unidas and going to junior high when I wasn't with all my friends with whom I had spent a long time. The Atotonilco schools were far away, but I adjusted. The scholarships helped us buy supplies, uniforms, and shoes, and pay for registration.

The English program was there at the beginning for me, and I liked the song about the parts of the body and teams with the names of vegetables and fruits. It was difficult, but I learned nouns, verbs, and pronouns. I was always excited for Wednesday with its many beautiful moments that I spent with the teachers. The Learning Center with the computers and Wi-Fi where I worked, helped me with my schoolwork.

ALFREDO

What I liked most about growing up in Los Ricos de Abajo was the freedom I was allowed and the tranquility of being able to see clear skies and sunsets, and to enjoy the rain.

Viaje al Centro de la Tierra by Jules Verne is my favorite book, and my least favorite is *La Perla* by John Steinbeck—I was assigned to read it at least five times and it became repetitive and not at all interesting. Literature has often inspired me, however, and I remember reading in English class about someone who dreamed big since childhood, and as an adult, he sought to fulfill those dreams and he fulfilled them. I learned that there are no impossible dreams or goals.

LAURA JIMENA

My favorite teacher at Naciones Unidas was Lucha, my first- and second-grade teacher. I respect and admire her because she was the one who taught me to read and who supports all of us, even after we have graduated and even if she's no longer teaching there. If I could give her a gift, I would give her a day at Los Ricos to have a reunion with all her students and their parents who esteem her for being the best teacher. She is loved and missed so much.

When I was in school, many of my peers were sent to other schools to study. Many parents believed that teachers taught for a year and left due to the difficulty, especially when it rains, in even getting to the school. I was a graduate of Naciones Unidas: I believe the school does not make the student; the student makes the school.

If I could travel, I'd go to Chiapas because I would like to know the culture, languages, and the cultivation of coffee and its processing. Outside of the country, though, I'd go to Spain because I read a book called *The Alchemist* by Paulo Coelho. From what the book says, there are beautiful plazas, beaches, a desert, and I'd like to eat Spanish food. I would also like to go to the famous Rock of Gibraltar.

My favorite university experience has been the Agronomy Congress that took place at Universidad Tecnológica de San Miguel de Allende in November 2019. Several universities attended, and the professors spoke of their professions and research projects. Another was when they took us to Expo-Agroalimentaria in Irapuato, Michoacan. I also enjoyed the practicums in the greenhouses and our garden plots where we harvested what we had planted.

LETICIA

I was born in 1997 and until I started university, I lived in Los Ricos. Spending my childhood there was wonderful. I remember the tranquility of the rancho, the sound of the birds, the wind blowing quietly, and leaves moving slowly in the trees and then falling.

The happiest family moments were weekends when I made enchiladas and quesadillas with my aunts and my mother—I miss that food. I also loved Maestra Lucha's classes at Naciones Unidas. The unhappiest time was when

I suffered a bit of bullying. Another difficult time was when it rained a lot—I went to the high school CBTis.60 in San Miguel and had to travel back and forth from Los Ricos to San Miguel—and the roads became slippery. But without a doubt, I would not change anything, nor would I forget anything because those experiences made me the person I am now.

I don't remember the first time the English program came to Los Ricos because right about then, I had started attending school in San Miguel, but I studied English on the weekends in the house of Señor Doug. The foreigners—the English teachers—are friendly, charismatic, and wonderful people. The first time I went to the classes I was nervous about all the unknowns, but in time I began to love it. Señor Doug always made us feel welcome.

I first met Linda Van Doren in the Saturday classes—another charismatic and friendly English teacher—and she became my friend. I trusted her deeply and remember that she was the first person who helped me and understood the fear that I felt about my sexual orientation. She was the first one who knew. Without a doubt, she was an especially important person in my life whom I'll always remember with a big smile.[5]

The scholarship I received was immensely helpful. I'm from a family of few resources, and I dare to say that without the scholarship I would not have continued my studies if it weren't for the beautiful angels that God placed in our path.

If I could go back in time and talk to the little girl from high school, I would tell her not to be afraid, everything would be fine, to study what makes her happy, and to challenge herself because she is capable of doing whatever is presented to her. With the passage of time, she will discover that she should value the things and people that she has at her side. Life teaches us many things, and nothing is certain, nothing is forever, nor is life itself safe, that a person is not valued for his money but because of his humility and his values. We are all worth the same because no matter what you have or do not have, in the end, all those are only material things.

MARÍA JOSÉ

I went to school at the Santuario in Atotonilco until the fourth grade. I have good memories of Naciones Unidas—a teacher named Pedro teaching me math, and the English teachers bringing in a hot-air balloon to Los Ricos where we could all get in. That's one of my best memories, but not everything

---

[5] Linda Van Doren died of cancer in 2016.

is pretty. I had few friends, and it seemed the only time girls and boys talked to me was to say something about my physique. Eventually, I changed over time and learned not to let those experiences ruin what were beautiful moments and memories of elementary school.

When I first saw the English teachers, I thought they were strange but kind people, and I didn't understand anything they said. But I enjoyed it so much that I didn't want them to leave. I wanted them to keep coming every Wednesday. The English classes helped because later we took English in high school, and it wasn't that difficult because I had already studied the language.

I really loved the food Feed the Hungry gave us in elementary school. The dishes were varied so we didn't always eat the same thing. Sometimes they didn't want to give us a double portion because they thought we wouldn't finish the food, but it was all varied with good nutrition.

When I started secundaria in Atotonilco, it was a big change since the subjects are more advanced. I made new friends quickly with classmates from other communities. The subjects that I liked the most were natural sciences, geography, and Spanish.

I remember well when the English classes started one January and the other girls from Los Ricos who were now at the university—Yessenia, Rosa Elena, and Aidé—came to talk with us. They told us what their studies were like, where they traveled, what they learned, and what it was like to try to get ahead, and not be left behind. They also said people, such as the English teachers, were there to support us, encourage us, and help us learn. I told myself that one day I, too, would stand in front of the students and talk about my experience, and I have done just that. I understand that elementary school students are looking only to what junior high will be like, but I want to tell the older students in high school to study, see the world, and what's going on, and not view it only from a desk.

The scholarships helped me a lot, starting in the seventh grade. They helped with my school fees, my school supplies, and shoes for the uniform. Now that I am at university, the support has helped me to keep pursuing my studies and to be a professional person as a graduate in business administration.

Now I see myself becoming a professional woman and traveling throughout the world. I don't know if I'll have a family or not, but I know that I'll always be a woman with a university degree.

AGUSTÍN[6]

I come from Mexico, home of the Aztecs, rich in cultural background. My state is Guanajuato or Quanaxhuato, the place where frogs live in Otomí. Otomí is the dialect of my hometown, Los Ricos de Abajo; it is my grandfather's language.

I spent the first eight years of my life with my father's family. It was there that I learned about my background and culture, especially from my grandfather. My grandfather was a hard worker who taught me the ways that my ancestors practiced agriculture, our traditional dishes, and most importantly, our native language. My grandfather offered the earliest motivation in my life and reminded me "Never forget where you come from, and you will achieve your goals." In this way, I learned to put my feet on the ground.

My father was my grandfather's reflection. He, too, was a hard worker and my most beautiful memory of him is when I spent every Sunday, his one day off, with him playing and watching outdoor soccer games the entire day. He showed me love and affection by including me in every activity, and this made me feel like the happiest child in the world. But when I turned eight years old, my father died, and my picture-perfect world was temporarily shattered. Nevertheless, the memory of my father continues to be my role model: he showed respect to everyone and helped people when they were struggling. The morning that he passed away, the last words that I heard from him were "Go to school."

Six years later—after the first English classes taught by volunteers at Naciones Unidas in Los Ricos—I moved to the United States. My goal was to come to New York City, make money for myself, and then live the rest of my life in Mexico. When I started to look at this new world, I saw that it was hard to live without education. I began to compare my life in New York with my life in Mexico and I noticed the opportunities in the United States were greater. I began to take advantage of every opportunity available. One day, my aunt said, "Agustín, I want you to go to school. I don't want you to live a life without a future." I was only fourteen years old. I was thinking like every teenager and only wanted to have fun, but little by little I started to open my eyes and remembered the teachings of my grandfather and my father: "People who don't have an education will be stuck in the same place forever." The older I got, the more I realized how true that statement was. Six months later my aunt registered me in school. My first experience in school was not a

_____

[6] A College Entrance Essay. Adapted from an article written by Agustín in the Washington Association for Language Teaching, 2015.

good one. I was treated like an outcast. People ridiculed me and made fun of the way I spoke. I cried every day after school. I knew crying was not going to solve anything so I braced myself and prepared for the journey ahead because I knew it would not be easy.

From that day on, my desire to learn grew stronger. I knew that I needed to apply myself more in school because I had a language barrier. The words of my grandfather constantly echoed in my ear; I remembered one day with him in the open field, and we were taking care of his animals, cows, and donkeys. He told me a story that his grandfather told him many years ago in the same spot that we were, under a little mesquite tree, where my great-grandfather practiced the agriculture taught by his ancestors. He had found something under that tree: a bag full of coins of silver! He took one and his grandfather made him put it back. "If something is not yours, don't touch it until you earn it." And my grandfather told me if you want to have fun, work hard until you deserve it.

In New York, I started to realize that my grandfather's stories weren't just about farming; he was talking about every aspect of living. That's why if the United States is giving me the chance to keep moving ahead with my studies, I should pay back by making my contribution be the best I can.

IN HER OWN WORDS: YESSENIA BALTAZAR RAMÍREZ

There are people who lament living in such a place as Los Ricos de Abajo. They say we suffer, live with limitations and no opportunities, surrounded by people who fight. That's what they say when they don't appreciate the beauty of being born in a community full of animals, plants, and beautiful land-scapes, or if they haven't learned to love the land where they were born, or if they sell the land inherited by their parents, land that their families worked on generation after generation.

Our childhood wasn't easy, but at the same time, it was wonderful. We started working from a young age in the fields. To do that, we had to get up at six in the morning to feed the cows that belonged to Pedro, my dad's cousin. He had a house in the country but lived in the city, so we took care of his cows and horse. When both my brothers and I finished this work, we ran back home, and then my sisters and I—or sometimes even all five of us—

went to the mill at Doña Graciela's house with our buckets of nixtamal.[7] She had a device that worked with gasoline and made the process of converting nixtamal into tortilla dough easier. Later we took it home for my mother to prepare tortillas. Doña Graciela had a schedule to grind the nixtamal and, if we didn't arrive at the right time, we had to go with my grandmother, Salud,[8] to grind the nixtamal in a hand mill where the energy used was our own.

Definitely more tiring. That's why we always tried to be at Graciela's on time.

After that, we had breakfast and went to school. After school, we ate at home and then it was back to the fields to take Uncle José's horses to the Río Laja where they drank the river water. We also cleaned the corral for Pedro's cows, filled their drinking troughs, and fed them. When we returned home, we would cut the kernels off the corn or help with housework and then do our homework. If we had time and if our father gave us permission, we could play with our cousins or sometimes they would play at our house. Our playmates were usually Alejandro and his brothers, and we had fun playing hide and seek, Encantados,[9] soccer, baseball, cops and robbers. They also had to work in the fields with their father so sometimes we played only in the afternoons. Usually, we worked while singing songs that we listened to on the radio or on the cassettes that my mom and dad had, and later their CDs.

When school wasn't in session, we went with Benigno to plant corn, pumpkin, and beans, which we liked doing. We also enjoyed going behind the yoke and throwing seeds: a corn, a bean, and a pumpkin. My grandfather said that each groove should have three grooves: the grandfather, the father, and the son. We had fun learning from him. Sometimes he had a stern character and always told us stories with a moral. Before planting corn, it was time of la rastra—that's when the land was prepared to lie fallow by removing the soil, not completely but enough so that we could dredge it with a team of horses that dragged leafy branches over the tilled land. We loved climbing all over

---

[7] Corn soaked in an alkaline solution that's ready to become hominy, masa dough, tamales, or corn tortillas. Ground nixtamal is typically referred to as masa.

[8] Salud's parents spoke Otomi. When they did the Calvary walk during the Lenten season and said their prayers, they used that language.

[9] Encantados is a game that consists of two teams. One team chooses a place (tree, lamppost, corner of a house, a stone) as their base. The other team has no base and must wait for the first team to leave their base. Then they run after them to touch them and yell "Encantado." That person cannot move until a teammate comes along to say "Desencantado." When every member of the team was Encantado and is now Desencantado, the roles of the team change.

the branches and when the horses pulled them, it was like riding on a sled. Pure adrenaline.

The most difficult and least fun was the corn harvest; we had to get up early and start the part called cegar: that was when we cut the corn plant from the lowest part of the main stem with an instrument called a hoz or sickle, like a curved machete. Then we could put all the corn plants together and make way for what's called the pinch of the cob, la pizca de la mazorca.

We worked quickly because as soon as the sun warmed the corn leaves, they became dangerous and could cut our hands. We made piles of stubble, and the mice came to make their nests and steal the corn. We had to harvest the beans before they were dry and we'd put them on blankets and hit them repeatedly, what we'd call varear. Afterward, the winds helped clean the beans, and then we'd put them in a tub—the tubs used to be made of aluminum but now they're plastic. When the beans were clean, we put them in sacks that my grandfather put in an old church[10] that they used as a warehouse to store beans and corn. The pumpkins were cooked, and we ate (or drank) them with milk, but others we split in two, took the seeds, and let them dry. After that, we roasted them on a comal[11] with salt and they were delicious. Sometimes we were in charge of gathering horse manure, which was bought by Luis, my mother's brother. I miss all that.

My mother taught us to draw flowers and weave napkins; to do so, she bought threads of many colors and an embroidery hoop. She also taught us to

---

[10] Edificación del siglo XVIII y XIX. Tras la fundación de San Miguel el Grande por fray Juan de San Miguel, en los pueblos cercanos a esta ciudad se establecieron varias capillas, las cuales captaron en su estructura e identidad, rasgos de templos de mayor dimensión, representaciones de santos o hechos propios de la religión impuesta, así como calvarios, calvaritos o humilladeros, ubicados en el exterior (de los que se dice estaban dedicados a los espíritus de quienes murieron de forma trágica y también a los que la gente suele "pedir permiso" previo a una festividad para evitar contratiempos), pero también se muestra parte de la visión indígena reflejada en las pinturas de los interiores de algunas capillas que representan "la flor de los cuatro vientos o rumbos", que para los otomíes es el símbolo de los cuatro dioses poderosos, o bien, con la figura de Edahi, el dios del viento o representaciones del Sol y de la Luna. https://www.mexicodesconocido.com.mx/ruta-capillas-indios-san-miguel-allende-guanajuato.html This old chapel is not in the Ruta de Capillas, but the architecture is similar. In Los Ricos de Abajo there are three such chapels: one belongs to the community, one is located within my uncle's land that once belonged to my grandfather, and another within another private property.

[11] A comal is a smooth, flat griddle typically used in Mexico, Central America, and parts of South America to cook tortillas and arepas, toast spices and nuts, sear meat, and generally prepare food. Similar cookware is called a budare in South America. Some comals are concave and made of barro (clay). Wikipedia.

grind in the metate.[12] I loved it when she made us atole de masa.[13] To this day, I love atole de maza with capirotadas.[14] My grandmother, Salud, also taught me how to weave.

When I was young, my father was a good father, and we sowed his land together. It was risky because rattlesnakes loved these lands, and once by accident my sister Sonia caught a baby rattlesnake. Luckily nothing happened but it managed to panic her. I loved seeing snakes, and my uncle Moises taught me how to catch them alive without being harmed. My father worked wherever he could, knew how to build houses, knew about electricity, or he filled carts with sand at the Río Laja for construction material.

When there was no work, he sold firewood, nopales, and potting soil, or in the rainy season, we would hunt for edible mushrooms and sell them. My father—and sometimes my mother—also collected honey and even when the bees stung him and made his face and eyes swell up, it didn't seem to bother him. I helped only when there were no more angry bees. I remember that when he came home from work tired, I helped him remove his boots and sat on his lap while we waited for the food that Mom was preparing.

On weekends we all went to the river or the countryside to spend the day chasing rabbits or getting honey from the bees. My father sang, no matter what he was doing, and from him, we learned to do the same. If we didn't feel like singing, we whistled. We were healthy children, and, in fact, I didn't put a foot in a hospital until I was 18.

Then one day, everything changed. My parents started fighting, and my father started drinking. In the beginning, his consumption was moderate, but with the passage of time, it increased. At our house, we had a huge garden and many fruit trees, so much fruit that when my aunts came to visit, they left with our excess fruit. But when my dad changed, the plants began to wilt and little by little the garden stopped being fertile, and no matter how much my mother wanted to save the garden, there was little she could do, just like with her marriage.

---

[12] In traditional Mesoamerican culture, metates were typically used by women who would grind lime-treated maize and other organic materials during food preparation. They are still popular today.

[13] Atole de masa is a traditional hot corn- and masa-based beverage of Mesoamerican origin. Wikipedia.

[14] Capirotada, formally known as "Capirotada de vigilia," is a traditional Mexican food similar to a bread pudding that is usually eaten during the Lenten period. It is one of the dishes served on Good Friday. Wikipedia.

My mother had a lot of strength, but I'm speaking of this other type of strength called resilience. Some people told her that she had to put up with her husband because marriage vows were until death do you part, that she couldn't raise five children by herself, and that alcoholism was a disease that she needed to accept.

Divorce was still not accepted and was synonymous with failure for which women are blamed. She was raised to serve a man, do her duty at home, and told to get those ideas out of her head. I know it was difficult for her. I even know that she suffered when they told her that I was not behaving well, that I shouldn't always be with my brothers, that she shouldn't let me go horseback riding or climb trees, and that I should be like other girls my age who had already learned to cook. They said that I was always running from one place to another, that my hair wasn't combed or clean, that I didn't wear shoes, and that as a woman, I would have no future. In their minds, a woman had a future if she learned to cook and do housework with the sole purpose of finding a husband and serving him well. But from my mother I learned what mattered most was, among other things, to be respectful, tell the truth, accept the consequences of my actions, be responsible, humble, say thank you and please.

When I was in the second year of school, things were not going well at home, and Maestra Lucha knew about the problem that my father was developing with alcohol and knew that the situation at home was economically difficult. She did her best to get me a scholarship for being an intelligent girl.

The years passed, and somehow, I survived. My parents fought, and when this happened, we would live for a while at my maternal grandparents' house, but then my parents would reconcile, and we'd go home. Back and forth.

We went to the hills to collect firewood, and sometimes when we did our homework, we had to do it in the dark because we had no light on my house. I was sad and ashamed that I had to do work by candlelight, but now I'm proud to say that.

Although I had few luxuries and a lot of homework, I still had fun with my brothers and had the best grades in school.

I knew that my mother did her best to take care of us by selling tortillas so that we could eat. Catalina Patlán and others[15] were a great support for Mom because they were the main buyers and helped her in any way they could. What I did to help my mother was take responsibility for myself by washing all my clothes and my blankets and leaving my room clean and orga-

---

[15] Daniel (Elena's uncle) and Cristina (a former neighbor in Los Ricos).

nized before going to school. I helped to make tortillas, just like my sisters, and when I received the scholarship, I bought something for the house or my personal things. I also started working on weekends in Atotonilco with my preschool teacher, Guadalupe Muñoz. Then later my godparents, José de Jesús Licea and Josefina Ramírez Mejía, asked me to take care of their grand-children and run their religious-goods store.

The first divorce process that I recall was in 2006 when I was ten years old. As I remember, it took place at the Courts or the Public Ministry on Colonia Guadalupe in San Miguel. We spent long hours waiting for the state-ment to be taken and during that time I saw the lawyers. They seemed to me to be extremely intelligent people and I had the opportunity to speak with one and from there, my passion for the law began. I saw women, so sure of themselves, well dressed, women different from those I knew who stayed at home. It awakened in me a desire to know more about the law. I admired the fancy legal books in their offices that contained information that I would later understand was difficult to read and comprehend. I thought it would be amazing to be a lawyer, and to this day, I still say that it is amazing to be one.

Then there was a major event in my childhood that made the difference between life and death. A day I remember perfectly well. I was in my room and my parents started to fight. My father was drunk and angry, and he started hitting my mother.

My sisters, like so many other times, tried to help my mother, but then he beat them, too. They ran to my maternal grandmother's house to get help. Meanwhile, my brothers tried to get him to release my mother, but in the same way, they were beaten. I just watched hoping that soon my father would leave my mother alone and then they would be happy again. By this time, my father, my mother, and I were the only ones in the house. He took her by the hair and dragged her across the patio.

When I saw him squeezing her throat, I realized he wasn't going to leave her alone, so I said, "! Ya, padre, deje a mi madre!" "Enough, Father, let go of my mother." I repeated it several times, but he didn't let her go. Over and over, I said it, and then I began to cry for everything, for my father, for my brothers and sisters, for my mother, and cried, "Ya, papi, suelte a mi mami, por favor." "Daddy, leave my mommy alone." He released her and told me: "Ya, hija, no llores, ya la solté." "OK, daughter, don't cry, I let her go." Then he left the house. A few minutes later, Mother's brothers arrived and took her to San Miguel to, I assume, file a complaint and both my brothers went to DIF to do the same.[16]

Later, after granting so many pardons and giving my father so many opportunities, my mother obtained a divorce in September 2011.

After going through that process, I sort of separated myself from the family.

Although I had witnessed the events, I did not want to be a part of them, and there was no human power that could force me to change my mind. My mother and my brothers believed that I did not love them and that I was in favor of my father and for a time they were upset. I understood them. I even understood my mother when she said she didn't love me because I knew she didn't mean it. I understood that she was going through enormous pain, fighting my father whom she loved so much, trying to take care of her children, dealing with legal proceedings, facing the people who gossiped about her and who said that she was a bad woman for not staying with an alcoholic. Truth is, she was never a bad woman; on the contrary, she is, and she will always be the best of mothers.

Neither parent is a bad person; they simply didn't know how to control their emotions or how to disagree without having to resort to shouting and hitting. I was neither for nor against them or the divorce. I had just had enough. I told them that I didn't want to participate in the divorce procedure—if you are going to get divorced, do it, I told them. It wasn't healthy for me to repeat over and over what I had witnessed—that was the procedure those days and they asked you, a million times over, to recreate the scene until they decided they had enough. (Currently, minors attend only a psychological evaluation and thank God, the authorities understand that children should not be much involved in these matters.)

Instead of living at home, I had started living in Atotonilco with my godparents, a couple who used to have a farm in Los Ricos which is where my parents met them and chose them as my godparents. I ended up working with them for six years selling religious goods in their stand in front of the church. They are like parents to me.

Thanks to them, I traveled to places like León, San Luis Potosí, San Juan de Los Lagos. Although I lived with them for a long time, I spoke little (really, with them I was a quiet and calm girl), but they were always there to give me good advice, even though I did not always follow it. I spoke little, but I

---

[16] The National System for Integral Family Development (Sistema Nacional para el Desarrollo Integral de la Familia; SNDIF or just DIF) is a Mexican public institution of social assistance that focuses on strengthening and developing the welfare of Mexican families. Wikipedia.

observed a lot. I could see that they lived differently.

José, my godfather, had a happy character and does to this day. He loves animals, too, and back then they had a squirrel and a parrot. He got a kick out of the parrot that would whistle at women and then follow that up by saying he was an ugly parrot and *joto* or gay.

My godmother, Josefina, was good with bookkeeping and at remembering the prices of everything sold in their store and a good businesswoman with imagination when it came to designing figures of alfeñique (confection molded from sugar paste) made the months preceding The Day of the Dead.

In their marriage, there were no arguments or at least they were never disrespectful to each other. Maybe things bothered them, but I never heard them fighting the way my parents did. No machismo, either. My godfather cooked and washed clothes, and my godmother taught me how to play dominoes and chess. They affectionately called me "Eyi" and teased me by saying things I hadn't said. It was wonderful to live with them. Working with them was fun, too, either braiding to make scapulars, assembling pictures, fixing rope, and sticking stamps to the image of the Señor de la Columna[17] or making a flag. Always something funny to make me laugh or to liven up the work. Sometimes I played with their grandchildren, Cris and Alex, or took them to the circus in Atotonilco.

When my godmother was recuperating from surgery, someone had to change her bandage, and I was always there with her to hold her arm because I believed that this would help her feel less pain. I loved her and I still love her and my godfather. I will always treasure the honor I had of knowing them. My godparents also employed my mother and brother on weekends and, although they didn't work long with them, they were treated well.

I went to Los Ricos once a week to see my mother. When I did go, I fought with my brother, and I think it was his way of saying that he was upset that I had abandoned him—we had been playmates—but our lives had radically changed. We no longer did what we liked. I cried sometimes when I was with my godparents because I missed the fun we had in the fields. I consoled myself by thinking that on vacation I could go to the fields to work the land with my grandfather, but unfortunately, he died, and the land was never planted again with the kind of work and love he gave it.

---

[17] The statue of El Señor de La Columna is in the Santuario de Atotonilco church and is sculpted out of Chichimeca materials such as corn stalk, corn starch, and powdered orchid bulbs. The image depicts Christ leaning against a column, dressed in a white loincloth, and has the kiss of Judas present on his cheek.

Now my uncles hire a tractor driver to do all the work. Part of the land was sold, and my grandfather's big house was divided. My aunts now live apart and have filled the land with fences. After my grandfather died, my grandmother, Salud, took refuge in alcohol, just as my father did. She used to be a wonderful cook, but she no longer is.

My best friend in secundaria was Estela, a true friend who was always there to help, listen to my sadness. We also accompanied each other in our mischief, such as escaping to the Río Laja and making food to take down to the river to eat.

I also had another friend named Claudia who taught me to play basketball in Atotonilco. Sometimes, when my godparents let me go to the park with her, we listened to songs and played. She nicknamed me Incesante because I didn't let anything stop me, I always had to be doing something; I did not tire easily. Sometimes we would go together to the Atotonilco fair in July when there is a fiesta in honor of Jesús Nazareno and we had fun on the wheel of fortune, flying chairs, pirate ships, and the Montaña Rusa (roller coaster).

One day Feed the Hungry arrived at our school with a woman who spoke Spanish and English—Olivia was her name—and we told each other that someday we would speak Spanish and English like Olivia.[18] I don't know how it began or how it was that Feed the Hungry decided to give English classes, but it was wonderful! How we waited to finish our regular classes and take English classes—a huge fascination.

I'm not the only one who remembers with special affection and love our first beloved teacher, Jackie Donnelly, who taught the fifth and sixth grades. We all loved her. Proof of this was that when she announced her farewell, we all felt sad and some cried. When we were introduced to our new teacher, we all, without exception, became rebellious. We made the new teacher suffer by screaming Jackie, Jackie, and we refused to remain silent and obey her. I understand that it was cruel to the new volunteer teacher, but we wanted Jackie with us at all costs. We missed her singing the songs like "Head, Shoulders, Knees, and Toes." Her spirit infected us all with joy. Before she left, she had an emotional talk with me. The best thing about sincere hugs is that they stay in the soul and transmit peace and joy. When she left, I made a promise to fulfill all my goals and dreams. Even back then, I knew I wanted to be a lawyer.

The English classes at Naciones Unidas helped us so much in secundaria that my teacher, Guadalupe, was interested in knowing how it was possible

---

[18] Professor Olivia Muñíz Rodríguez has been part of Feed the Hungry almost since the beginning. She is the meals program director.

that Elizabeth and I were advanced in English. We told her about the teachers in Los Ricos and she and the school director wanted to meet them. Even though we had graduated from elementary school, the English classes hadn't ended. On Wednesdays, we went to our old elementary school in the afternoon to take more classes. Señora Dianne's husband, Señor Tom, handed out cookies and juice, always smiling and saying in English: Would you like some cookies? Would you like apple juice or orange juice?

One of my English teachers was Cathy Scherer, who taught with her heart. Geoff Hargreaves taught Elizabeth and me and further developed my taste for literature and my desire to write. His class dealt with the works of Shakespeare sometimes and it was fun. Other times we described people we talked with, and I still have some of the notebooks from his class. He gave me some books, magazines, and an English deck of cards. He also helped a lot with the process of choosing a university.

During my high school studies, the Los Ricos English teachers set up the Learning Center, a computer center in the Naciones Unidas Elementary School. Without it, we could not have done the excellent work we did in high school. I was fortunate to manage it with my best friend, Maritza Ramírez. We were responsible for opening the Learning Center three days a week and monitoring compliance with the rules, for which we received a double scholarship. In addition, the English teachers paid our tuition at the Instituto Illescas on Saturdays. In 2016, I graduated as a Systems Designer which has helped me a lot because I learned about the use of computers and various programs. While I worked in the Learning Center, I could also do my high school homework and that of the Instituto Illescas.

Shortly before leaving high school, Maritza and I taught summer courses at the San Miguel de Allende Public Library. We met many children who treated us with great love and even gave us cupcakes. We learned that it was lovely being a teacher, but we were still clear: I wanted to be a lawyer and she wanted to study Graphic Design.

When I finished high school, I also stopped working with my godparents in Atotonilco because I wanted new challenges. From then on, my life would change even more. I remember that, during a psychological visit with the NGO Jóvenes Adelante's psychologist Jorge, he told me that I was clear about my goals, but that I was naive and that, over time, I would learn not to trust people so much, and that's what happened.

I was accepted to receive the Jóvenes Adelante scholarship for university students if I managed to get into the Universidad de Guanajuato (UG), so I started the admission process and was always supported by Geoff, Doug,

Dianne, and her husband. The first time I went to turn in my documents, Dianne and Tom took me to the capital city, Guanajuato, where I had been once before. After handing in my documents, getting the ID to take the exam, and finishing the tour of the university, they took me on a tour of the city while Dianne told me how it was in 1992 when she was on sabbatical and first visited Guanajuato. The tour ended with a good meal in Casa Valadez in the Jardin Unión, and I fell more in love with Guanajuato. I already imagined living there and studying at UG, so I put in a lot of effort studying.

On the day of the exam, Dianne and the teachers' program hired Gregorio Sierra Diaz to drive to Los Ricos de Abajo to pick me up early in the morning and take me to Guanajuato to take the exam. I was surprised that day to see that there were more than 400 applicants doing the same, among them was Fanny whom I would meet later.

The school sent me the exam results via the internet without correcting the test and instead sent me an option to take a preparatory course and to take the exam again next year. I did not take propedeutico. I was sad and angry, and could not believe that I had not been accepted.

The volunteer teachers sent me words of encouragement and later Geoff told me that Universidad Allende wanted me to study there on a scholarship and they wanted an interview with me. So I entered the Universidad Allende.

In June 2014, I went to work at the artisans' shop which didn't work well as the owner refused to pay me. I was beginning to see the truth in Jorge's warning. However, I got another job at a gallery where I worked until I entered the university. She asked me to continue working after my university classes started.

My time at the university was the most difficult part of my life. I always had words of encouragement from the volunteer teachers. Classes at the university began and I met new colleagues who lived in another world, most from the city and not from rural communities like mine. I no longer had any close friends. I didn't know anyone at the Universidad Allende, and I didn't talk much with my classmates because I thought we had nothing in common. During the break, I would lock myself in the university library or stay in the classroom to do my homework because right after school, I had to go to the Instituto Municipal de la Mujer to do tee social service work required by the university as a scholarship student.

Here I also met great people, and we became a great team. At that time, I knew little about the law, and at times, they would let me read the law books that they had in the office. After that, I had to go to the public library for books that I needed. When the books I needed weren't in the library, Doug provided me with money from the teachers' program to buy them. I tried not to bother him too much because I wanted to make the effort myself. After I went to the library, I went to work at an art gallery; sometimes it was too late for me to return to Los Ricos, so I had to sleep at the owner's house.

In September 2014, everything was going well at the university despite being the only one in the group who was attending school on a scholarship and who had to work after school while the rest went to the gym or the cafeteria. I didn't care. I was clear about my goals and objectives, and I had the support of the volunteer teachers closest to me. Nancy Zimmerman gave me some of her clothes so that I could look the way our teacher required us to dress—like lawyers.

Señor Geoff was always attentive to my grades and my attendance at the university and when on September 22, 2014, I had an incident that forced me to be in the hospital for the first time. I had to stay in bed for weeks and could no longer continue studying. Thanks to Señor Geoff, I went back to the university—I didn't want to disappoint him. He trusted me a lot and asked that I be allowed to take the exams. I went back to school, but it was difficult because sometimes, out of nowhere, I wanted to cry.

I did take the second Universidad de Guanajuato exam to be accepted. Nothing. The same results.

But then a change occurred—a person started classes with me who would become my best friend, Estefanía Godínez Elias (Fanny). She was always looking for a way to start a conversation with me, difficult at the time because I had become remote and separate from others. But little by little we became friends. We told each other how we took the exam on two occasions to enter UG—turns out that twice we were in the same auditorium, but we didn't know it until we met at the Universidad Allende.

I was still living in Los Ricos, and it was difficult to get to the university on time because there were no buses leaving the community early enough.

Maritza was now studying at the Instituto San Miguelense and the two of us spent much of our time walking and riding on buses. One day one of the English teachers decided to lend us her house in Las Cuevitas, a San Miguel colonia. This made everything much less difficult for us, even the schoolwork was easier—we had internet at the house—and I had more time to read or go running. The house was comfortable, and we were able to have breakfast and get to class on time.

Later Maritza, Rosa Elena, and I moved to an apartment on Calle Potrerito in Colonia Santa Julia. Feed the Hungry's English teachers rented it for us, paid the expenses, and furnished it. It felt like a real home. I almost didn't really live with them because I came home late from working at the gallery, but when I could get there early, we cooked together, had dinner, and talked about our day. It was a lot of fun, and we were happy studying, among friends.

Maritza left us soon with enormous sadness. We wanted to help her stay in school, but she took a different direction. She would be a mother.

Before I took the second exam at the Universidad de Guanajuato, Nancy Zimmerman recommended that I talk with a lawyer and notario[19] to see if he could help me in the admissions process. He gave me good advice and said that no matter what happened, I should start working in some law firm because the practice would help me. I ended up following his advice by obtaining an internship with a lawyer. Señor Doug gave me the contact information of a lawyer, Gabriel García McFarland, and told me about him. I wrote an email to Gabriel to schedule an interview and he gave give me the opportunity to work in his office as a law intern. I am grateful to Doug because without his recommendation, Lic. Gabriel would not have offered me that position. I started working on July 7, 2015, and the experience helped me a lot. Lic. Gabriel is a bilingual lawyer and most of the clients didn't speak Spanish, so the English classes with Señor Doug helped me immensely to answer questions and schedule appointments when Gabriel was left without a bilingual secretary.

But still, around that time, I decided to leave the university because I didn't understand the behavior of some classmates. The classroom had become a battlefield. Students were divided. Some of us felt we had more values and had a concept of empathy that was different from the others who had Machiavellian ideas. The atmosphere was extremely tense. We also had a teacher who sometimes didn't teach.

With all that going on, I decided that I didn't want to continue.

I had also decided to open a business which failed but I didn't want to talk to anyone about it either because the failure hurt. The only person I confided in was Estefanía who felt bad for not being able to do anything to convince me to come back to law school. The university had been a roller coaster. When I started, I did so with all my determination and hopes, but suddenly external factors caused me to want to resign.

When the volunteer English teachers found out what I was thinking, they tried to make me see that it was important not to forget my dreams. We had a meeting at Señora Dianne's house with Lic. Gabriel and other volunteer teachers. After that talk, I decided that I wanted to return to the university,

---

[19] A notary (or notario) in Mexico has similar functions to a United States notary, but the importance and power that a notary has in Mexico are much greater.

but I would study only on Saturdays and during the week I would work with Lic. Gabriel.

They also reminded me how strong I was. On one occasion when I asked for advice from Señora Dianne, she answered me with a true and important phrase: "What doesn't kill you makes you stronger."[20] It was the end of the race. I was about to accomplish my dreams, but at the same time, I was saying to Señora Dianne that I was tired. She also gave me the option to pamper myself with a prize at the end of the week or after a long day of work. It worked! I gave myself an ice cream or a chocolate. I would dance or go running because I deserved a healthy distraction.

In September 2017, my father was hospitalized in the Hospital General de San Miguel de Allende with subdural hematoma. I was taking care of him and stopped attending school. I fell behind in my classes and couldn't graduate that year. The school allowed me to return, but on May 22, 2018, my father went into a coma. He was low in platelets due to his alcohol problem, and they couldn't operate on him.

The doctors said that if he had surgery, he had zero chance of survival. I was at a crossroads where I had to decide to disconnect him or fight for his surgery. I will not judge people, each one has different ways of thinking and acting, but a doctor who already knew me and had cared for my father told me to disconnect him so that I could continue to live. I would always have to take care of him, and I deserved to live my own life without worrying about him. It would not be a crime, he said, because the only reason my father was living was that they had him hooked up to thousands of devices. If he woke up, he would never be the same, perhaps he would not remember anything, and he would not have mobility on his own.

A big dose of reality, but I refused to disconnect. The next day my uncle was admitted to the hospital, to the same room as my father, and the day after, my uncle died. I decided to take my father to Irapuato for the operation. I didn't have the heart to disconnect him.

Once in Hospital General de Irapuato,[21] I didn't want to leave the waiting room even though there was a hostel or albergue nearby. When the doc-

---

[20] "What doesn't kill you, makes you stronger" comes from an aphorism of the nineteenth-century German philosopher Friedrich Nietzsche. It has been translated into English and quoted in several variations but is generally used as an affirmation of resilience. Dictionary.com.

[21] Irapuato has a population of 529,440. Wikipedia. It is 104 kilometers from San Miguel de Allende.

tors finished the neurosurgery to remove the subdural hematoma, they were going to take my father to intensive therapy. I outwitted the guards and just when the surgery was over, I got into the operating room. It was thoughtless on my part. I know that you must go into an operating room with gloves and all those special things to avoid an infection, but I wanted to see my father and know that he was fine. A moment of madness.

After I had assured myself that my father's surgery was successful, I was hungry, so I went to the street in search of a fonda and soon ate. Afterwards, my mother called me and said I should eat even if I wasn't hungry because if I didn't, I could get sick. I think that was the first time that my mother said something like that to me. I told her that I had already eaten and that my father was in intensive care. I also told her that I would sleep in the waiting room with other people, which is what I did; however, someone stole a cell phone in that room. My sleep was light because I didn't want to wake up and not have my things.

Fortunately, José Iván (who would become my best friend and then my husband) called me from Monterrey and kept the conversation going almost all night. Sometimes he had to hang up because he had to take care of his work in Monterrey, but he often talked about the city, how different life was there, how typical it was to eat carne asada, that hearing it sparked my interest in getting to know Monterrey. Even when his night work was over, he kept talking even though he would have to get up early to go to school.

By the next morning at six, my conversation ended with José Iván. I left the waiting room, had breakfast, answered some messages, and started to read *El Leviatán de Thomas*.[22] Then I went for some food and later I spoke to José Iván again; that day I did not see my father because I had to go to the Irapuato's center to buy a fan that he needed in the ICU. A woman approached me, and asked me if I was from Irapuato, and when I answered no, she asked how I was going to do it. Well, I said, I'll go downtown. Do you know how to get there? My answer was—no, pero preguntando, se llega a Roma, but by asking, anyone can get to Rome. She told me to be careful and take care of myself. It all

---

[22] *Leviathan or The Matter, Form and Power of a Commonwealth Ecclesiastical and Civil,* commonly referred to as *Leviathan,* is a book written by Thomas Hobbes (1588–1679) and published in 1651 (revised Latin edition 1668). Its name derives from the biblical Leviathan. The work concerns the structure of society and legitimate government, and is regarded as one of the earliest and most influential examples of social contract theory. Written during the English Civil War (1642–1651), it argues for a social contract and rule by an absolute sovereign. Hobbes wrote that civil war and the brute situation of a state of nature ("the war of all against all") could only be avoided by a strong, undivided government. Wikipedia.

worked out and I delivered the fan and other things that had been requested.

When night fell, many patients' families slept on the floor instead of going to a hotel or albergue because they wanted to be there in case their sick family member needed something. One family was asked for a lot of ice, which they managed to get. Again, my sleep wasn't heavy, and any sound made me alert. Before dawn, I was awakened by the sound of a woman asking for the family of a patient who had died, and it turned out to be the group that had bought all the ice. Their dreams were crushed, and they burst into screams.

I couldn't go back to sleep, so I found a spot in the outskirts of the hospital to read my book. It was then the ICU called me to find some ice. Ice! I ran for ice at a convenience store I had seen, but there was no ice. I ran to another store that turned out to be closed. A real adventure—I ran from place to place until I found some—made worse by my remembering that the family of the patient who died had also been asked for ice. I calmed myself by repeating something I had learned from studying law: Not all cases are the same, no matter how similar they seem.

Nothing serious happened and by noon I could go in and see my father, but he still hadn't awakened. But he was alive! The days passed and they were alike: José Iván called at dawn with our eternal phone calls, people died, and others came with patients. After so many days, I was so dirty that I decided to go to the albergue, but it was closed. They said that since nobody was using it, they had closed it, and it was too late. I decided that at night I would take a bath in the room where they kept cleaning supplies for the toilet. That night, I took two buckets, filled them with water, and took them to the service room and there I bathed. I wore the change of clothes that I had brought for my dad, and I washed mine in the bathroom sinks (the days had been so hot that I knew they would dry).

I hadn't started conversations with anyone during those days—the person I talked with was José Iván—but without my realizing it, people had watched me. One day while reading my book, a señora interrupted me to ask me to take care of her things while she went for a medicine that she had been asked to get, so I stopped reading and concentrated on taking care of her things. When she returned, she asked if no one would be coming to be with me. I answered that I had come from far away and didn't think anyone else would come. Maybe my father would wake up soon, I said. Then she told me that her son spent six months in intensive care and has been in the extreme care area for three months. She also said that most people had been there for more than a month because it isn't easy for someone to be released from the ICU. Many of the people there were destitute, and I began to wonder what happened to them to decide to live a life like this. There was a señora whose husband came to stay with her, and during the day when the señor went to work, the señora rarely ate. I decided to give her food, but she ate little and said she had no appetite. I remembered what my mother had told me days ago that I should eat. I think that in difficult situations most people lose their appetite, but since I was optimistic, I still had an appetite.

Little by little, I managed to get the señora to eat and I always tried to be with her during mealtimes so that she wouldn't stop eating. One day the señora broke down crying and hugged me. She asked me: "How do you not give up? I saw you arrive alone, and I saw that no one has come to see you. You manage alone without fear. We all saw that you bathed in the service room. All of us who sleep in the waiting room talk about how you bathe in such a small room with the help of two buckets. Every morning you get up as if you had lived here for a long time. You pick up your blanket, you go to the bathroom, you clean yourself, put on makeup, comb your hair, and go out to breakfast. Then you start reading, calling, visiting your patient, as if all this were normal for you, and I have not seen you cry."

I didn't know how to answer. I hadn't even noticed that when faced with adversity I behaved differently from others. The señora had observed me well and later another señora told me that I was too young to have so much control of my acts and emotions.

After two weeks, my father was transferred back to Hospital General de San Miguel where he spent a few days in intensive care. His recovery was gradual. Again, I was behind in school. Señora Dianne and the teachers offered to pay a nurse to take care of him, but I did not accept because my father is stubborn; he doesn't like hospitals or nurses, and behaves horribly when he's angry. It takes a lot of patience to take care of him. I'm the only one in my family who can tolerate doing it. José Iván kept calling me, but now by video call. He said that he had dark circles under his eyes and sometimes at dawn he fell asleep; I tried not to bother him much so that he wouldn't neglect his studies. My friend Fanny sent food to me in the hospital in the afternoons, Lety also brought me food, as did Francisco and Noria (two great friends).

When he recovered, I went back to school and to my job with Lic. Gabriel.

I don't know what changed during my stay at the hospital, but I knew that something had.

I remember a phrase by Gabriel García Márquez that says: "Human beings are not born forever the day their mothers give birth to them, but rather life forces them to give birth to themselves over and over again."[23] And that's what happened! It was like being born again, not only for me but for my father, because when he woke up it was difficult for him to move. For me, it was like having a baby, a big baby. I changed the sheets with the help of the nurse and helped him with the exercises that the therapists had taught him. When he recovered and the tube was removed, I had to change his diaper, take him to the bathroom, bathe him, and feed him.

But it was not only this process that was like being born again, but I realized that I had been doing it for a long time: since the divorce, when I went to high school, to university. Life and circumstances forced me to give birth to myself, to adopt new ways of life, and in each new birth, I was the only one responsible for choosing well.

I could take advantage of the processes of change to be a better person or let myself be led by circumstances and become a person who constantly blamed others for what happened. The second option is not a good one, nor will it ever be, and I am grateful that for some reason I am always reborn stronger, with less fear and more determination. I began to change. I valued myself more. When I returned from Irapuato, I no longer allowed people to be in my life who underestimated me, who made me feel bad.

When my father was discharged, my mother agreed that he return to the house in Los Ricos; she and my brothers would help take care of him. I returned to work with Lic. Gabriel and in the afternoons after work, I went to Los Ricos to help. My father did not fully recover his mobility, but he could fend for himself. He doesn't speak well, but you can understand him a little. A true miracle, they told me. But, once again, he took refuge in alcoholism. A person asked me: How could I not be upset about everything I did for my father, and he didn't value it? You should be angry with him, that person said. But I have no reason to be angry. Working through that situation was a big help to me. I did it from the heart because I love my father. When I did it, I didn't expect him to thank me.

I wanted to be alone, but I had found a perfect long-distance friend: José Iván who studied and worked in Monterrey. I hadn't known or didn't remember that we had been together in secundaria—in different classrooms—but he had remembered, and later that year when he was on school vacation, we became novios. I could tell he loved me by the way he dealt with me and

---

[23] "Los seres humanos no nacen para siempre el día en que sus madres los alumbran, sino que la vida los obliga a parirse a sí mismos una y otra vez." El coronel no tiene quien le escriba.

his way of expressing himself. It was fun talking with him. He already knew everything about me—and he was happy to be with me. But at the end of his vacation, he had to return to Monterrey, and I didn't stop him.

In September, I competed in an athletic competition in San Miguel de Allende called La Simbólica. José Iván came from Monterrey and surprised me by waiting for me at the race's finish line. I didn't win—I was in twelfth place—but it was significant that he was there. He stayed a month and then returned to Monterrey.

In November, it was the second time that I had an interview to obtain a visa, the first time in Mexico City and the second in Guadalajara. My plan was to go to Virginia to visit Cathy Scherer, one of my English teachers, who had offered me a three-month law internship in Virginia. I was excited to be able to travel, but I wasn't granted a visa. I did receive, however, kind messages from Señora Cathy and other teachers, something that I appreciated much.

In December, we found out I was two months pregnant. I refused to believe it. José Iván and I had talked about both of us finishing school and then we would travel. We didn't plan to have a family. Although I refused to believe it, several blood tests confirmed that, yes, it was true. I had to leave fear behind, but it wasn't easy. José Ivan felt guilty about the fact that I was expecting a baby because my life would change radically, and I would have to give up my plans. But I came to understand that guilt was useless.

For a long time, I had blamed myself for things that had not been in my hands. Now I told him that it wasn't his fault. It was destiny. We must take responsibility and accept the consequences, but without anyone being guilty. He left his studies and work in Monterrey. I didn't ask him to do that, even though I wasn't willing to leave either my studies or my work.

On January 26 of 2019, I finished my university studies and on the same day, we had a civil marriage. My husband prepared a small meal to celebrate my marriage, my birthday, and the conclusion of my university studies. In March 2019, my employer, Lic. García McFarland, partnered with a notario and while I'm not a notario, I learned to do things typical of one. In July, a week before giving birth, I left the job and promised to return as soon as I could.

My delivery was scheduled to be a normal delivery. In July, I started labor, but my baby stopped breathing, so they had to perform a cesarean section due to fetal risk. It was frustrating because during the pregnancy I did exercises to help have a normal delivery. Although I did not want a cesarean, life sometimes surprises us. After Xenia Ayleen was born, I received congratulatory messages from the teachers, and then went to Montecillo de Nieto with my husband. My mother-in-law took good care of me for two weeks. My husband gave me a book so that it would be less terrible to be recuperating.

I returned to work in September, and I was able to take my baby with me. She's a calm baby and lets me work. At work, I've met new people and sometimes they care for my baby. My best friend Estefania has been working since 2018 in the office too. They are all excellent people.

My relationship with my mother has improved. She understands that I love both her and my father equally and the fact that I spend more time with my father doesn't mean that I don't love her. On the contrary, it was because I love her so much that I decided at a young age to help her by taking responsibility for myself, for my expenses, for always maintaining good grades, for keeping my scholarship, and I have let her know that in many ways. I didn't want to see her suffer because, for me, she is a great woman who had to radically change her life and fight so that her children could eat. She also suffered after her divorce because people pointed out that she didn't stay at her husband's side. But I know that you cannot stay in a place where you know you will not be happy.

I am not always strong. I was afraid that my father's alcoholism might affect me in the future, so I spoke with Señor Doug, and he recommended that I attend a group where people meet who have an alcoholic relative in common: Al-Anon.[24]

Months later, in February 2020, I admitted my father to an Alcoholics Anonymous group for three months, and on Sundays I went to Querétaro to visit him, always accompanied by my baby. Before each visit, talks were held with the relatives of the alcoholics, and each time they chose someone to go up to the rostrum to talk about what they felt. When it was my turn, I didn't know how to start, but I started to speak anyhow and, in the end, I was crying. I realized that there was something in me that was not healing, something I needed to understand. The talks helped me a lot because I realized that I was feeling guilty for the half-life that my father led after neurosurgery. With the help of the talks, the advice of my husband and those of my best friend Fanny, I was cured of what I was not aware of: if my father had not entered the rehabilitation center for alcoholics, I would not have gone up to the rostrum, and I would not have talked about it, and I would not have realized that I suffered.

In May 2020, my father left the center, and although I hoped he wouldn't

---

[24] Al-Anon Family Groups is a worldwide fellowship that offers a program of recovery for the families and friends of alcoholics, whether or not the alcoholic recognizes the existence of a drinking problem.

get drunk anymore, he started once more. I talked to him and realized that he was still intelligent and remembered many things from when we were children. He said that he would drink again, I shouldn't let it bother me, it was his decision. I knew that if I could eliminate all the bottles of alcohol, he'd find more. He's happy like this, it is his life and his decision. I will always be there to extend my hand when he needs it. My husband told me that it was incomprehensible but admirable that despite everything I have done for my father, when he decided to drink again, I took it so lightly, but I told him what I have always done is try to understand my father, my mother, my brothers, everyone. For me, it has always been much better than judging and hating them. And so I am happy. Y así soy felíz.

Today after the passage of time, my mother and I are a little more united and our differences are in the past. My mother is a great woman who, despite all this, still stands with her head held high with goals and dreams. I know that she loves me and is proud of me. I'm sorry she doesn't tell me, but I know how she feels.

My husband and I are working to build our own house so that we can live in the rancho together, not with my in-laws but in a house of our own. I want to continue studying because I want to be a better lawyer and improve my English. My husband stopped studying but he is happy as a horse keeper on a ranch.

Sometimes we cannot spend the night together and, no, he does not have a wife who always cooks for him or does the things that wives do. But we both understand that we are free people who seek to share a life together without being tied to each other at every moment, without machismo, and without harm.

An old saying affirms that to educate a child you need a village. Although the primary education of the child is the responsibility of the parents, I was able to count on the moral and financial support of the volunteer teachers who have come to be almost a part of my village. They helped me broaden my horizons and grow in my own personality. Otherwise, with my absent parents and problems at home, perhaps I would not be who I am today. I learned not to be a victim. I am not a victim of my past. I am a survivor. Today, I embrace my past and I wouldn't change a thing.

I am infinitely grateful to the volunteer teachers who are and have come into my life. Having them was what helped me regain my sanity in difficult times when I needed a word of encouragement or a cup of chocolate, as Señor Geoff calls a snack, or una agüita de Jamaica with Señor Doug, an unexpected message from one of my great dear teachers, Jackie or Cathy, wise advice from

Dianne, and the unconditional help of the other volunteer teachers.

Many people have asked me, "Twenty-four years old and you are still not successful, and you have nothing?" They believe that being successful is having big houses, new cars, and a lot of money. I have a title of Systems Designer and a Law Degree. I also have five years of experience as a lawyer, thanks to Lawyer Gabriel García McFarland who opened the doors of his legal office and gave me a vast accumulation of legal experiences.

Thankfully, I have sixteen years of being independent of my parents during which time I have worked hard to cover my personal expenses and help my parents when possible. Many scholarships helped me along the way: one Maestra Lucha arranged for me when I was young, Mujeres en Cambio[25] assisted me after that, as did an award from the city government, and when those ended, the volunteer teachers at Los Ricos de Abajo stepped up. This help allowed me to study and fulfill two great dreams, to have more knowledge about computers and to become a lawyer. At this moment I consider myself a successful person who has fought for what I wanted. I owe my success to the volunteer teachers, my family, my godparents, my teachers and all the people who have been there to believe in me, to encourage me not to abandon my dreams. Thanks to them, today I have the necessary skills to face and create a better future for myself and for my new family, José Iván and our daughter Xenia.

---

[25] Mujeres en Cambio (Women in Change) from San Miguel de Allende is a legally established nonprofit organization run by volunteers committed to enhancing the lives of women living in rural communities near San Miguel de Allende, Gto, Mexico. Scholarships from Mujeres en Cambio enable rural girls to continue their education beyond grade school.

Maestra Lucha crossing what was left of the pedestrian bridge to school. Taken by a student and restored by Billie Mercer

Crossing the river before the vado was built . The vado became a reality by spring 2021.

Teacher/driver Doug Lord figuring out how deep the river is and the rocks he hopes to avoid

Lucha and the students repairing the road to the school

Naciones Unidas School. Years ago the nearby monastery, Monasterio de Señora de la Soledad, requested funds from international donors to build the school. Hence the name: Naciones Unidas. The English teachers often parked at the monastery when they had to look for alternative ways to cross the Río Laja.

Maestra Lucha

With help of donors and Feed the Hungry, a new comedor was built.

2011 The library has shelves! Students enjoying the library.

Old latrines and new toilets. With contributions from donors and Feed the Hungry, we hired an architect and paid the parents to build them.

Rick Hernández on the patio with students.

Teacher Jean Degnon and a student.

Students working on a computer in the Learning Center.

Program at Pro Música.

Students sharing library books.

Teacher Julie Preis keeping students engaged.

Students attending the San Miguel Writers' Conference

Traditional dancing at the fiesta for the volunteers

Left: Mother & daughter dancing at the final festival of our school year.

Traditional dancing at the closing fiesta for the volunteers.

Dianne with a Los Ricos mother.

Making the teachers' favorite mole for the end-of-our-year fiesta.

Doug Lord witnessing high school graduation. Photo: Billie Mercer

Maestra Lucha with Naciones Unidas mothers in the basket of a hot air balloon.

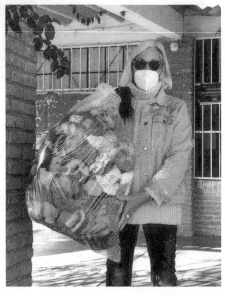

Doug with a graduating student.

During Covid, director Suzanne Bacon delivered gifts from the San Miguel Knitters.

Los Ricos de Abajo English Teachers in the Feed the Hungry warehouse.

Los Ricos de Abajo English Teachers

Los Ricos de Abajo English Teachers

Los Ricos de Abajo English Teachers

Part 4

GROWTH RESPONDS TO NEEDS

CHAPTER 11

Week to Week, Month to Month:

TEACHING FROM KINDERGARTEN TO ADULT

It's Wednesday afternoon at Los Ricos, a bright beautiful day in late January. A few wispy high clouds cut the intensity of the sun. Teachers have carpooled out to the school. Students have finished their lunch and come to welcome the teachers. A trusted student carries the key to the gate. As it swings open, our cars roll up to parking spaces past the few pieces of ancient playground equipment.

Amid smiles and greetings, "How are you?" teachers gather their satchels and boxes of necessary supplies carefully planned for the day's lesson. Bags contain clipboards with class lists and lesson plans. The lead teacher in each grade passes out copies of the lesson plan to fellow volunteers. Fellow teachers greet, chat, and are ready to head to the classrooms. The kindergarten volunteers are coming down from the kindergarten class just up the hill. Most will stay on for this session and lunch. Some will stay on teaching the junior and high schoolers as well.

The main school building is one story consisting of a first- and second-grade classroom, a third- and fourth-grade classroom, and a third room on the end which was a storage area that has been turned into the library. The fifth- and sixth-grade classroom was built a little later and is a separate structure connected by a cement sidewalk. The roof of the main building extends over a covered patio spanning the front of the building. There is a low wall around the perimeter of the patio which provides convenient seating. This building is typical of the construction of the area with cement posts and cross supports. The area in between is filled with bricks and mortar. The lighting comes from above where fiberglass panels in the roof let in natural light. The fifth- and sixth-grade classroom has windows along both sides which lets in plenty of bright daylight. Down a few steps across from the front of the building is the multipurpose basketball court. Here students line up by grade at the beginning of the day for opening exercises and are led by their teachers into class. We enjoyed watching many programs of student folk dances on this court on our final fiesta days. Here Lucha's retirement celebration ceremony was held.

Around the corner at the rear of the building is the Feed the Hungry kitchen. In the past, children collected their lunch at the window and sat on the patio wall to eat, which on some winter days could be windy and dusty. Not long after the program started, the volunteers, donors, and Feed the Hungry arranged for a dining room to be constructed. This room has long tables, built-in seating around the periphery and benches. The tables are covered with colored oil cloth. Here, the volunteers enjoy delicious comida prepared by the mothers. There is a small sink where children wash their hands before meals. After lunch, the dining room becomes a classroom for the high school students who return for tutoring from their school day in Atotonilco.

Over time, changes and improvements have been made to the school, mostly thanks to the volunteers and Feed the Hungry. Certainly, the addition of the flush toilets was an early improvement. Volunteers have done regular maintenance such as repairing broken windows. The substantial library space was used as a storeroom for a wheelbarrow, hoses, bags of cement and other building materials. The first order of business was to build a shed to house these supplies. This improvement was accomplished by hiring men from the village who are skilled construction workers.

Now the library has become a clean open room ready for the next steps. The large windows on three sides needed curtains to filter the hot afternoon sun. Sturdy Mexican cotton called manta was purchased and one of the mothers sewed the draperies. Shelves and books were brought from the States. Later, with the addition of used computers updated by Computadoras Pro Jóvenes and the addition of Wi-Fi, the library evolved into the Learning Center.

Our classroom supplies of notebooks, pencils, crayons, scissors, are kept in plastic tubs in the library. In the country schools, such supplies are coveted. Each grade has its tub of supplies, provided by the volunteers. Students are eager to fetch the tubs and take them to the classroom when teachers arrive. The basic desks are one piece, made of metal, with the seat and writing arm attached. A cubby beneath the seat holds the notebook, texts, and backpack. Students in the fifth and sixth grades have personalized the scarred writing surface, covering it with popular pictures of cartoon characters, princesses, trucks, animals, and superheroes, the whole surface wrapped in protective plastic.

Some changes were identified and made for the benefit of the volunteers. When we first started teaching at Los Ricos the sound of twenty metal desks scraping across the classroom concrete floor in the fifth- and sixth-grade classroom was a bit unnerving for the uninitiated. The problem was solved when a volunteer brought bags of spent tennis balls with an X cut in each one to allow the ball to be pushed onto the bottom of each desk leg. Each desk required four neon yellow balls. Now when the class formed into its groups there was a smooth transition. This small fix has lasted for years and is appreciated by the regular classroom teacher as well.

Upon arrival, volunteers from the United States and Canada may first notice what is lacking in the physical school. This feeling of deficit soon disappears when one sees what is there. There is the striking placement of the school facing east on the high point of the village. From the covered patio, one looks out to the view of fields, farmland, and the green foothills in the distance. The school compound is a little world unto itself and the children, their parents, and indeed the entire village feel pride in the school and a strong connection to it. Mothers, fathers, and grandparents attended this school. Grandfathers may have helped build the school. Fathers are involved in maintenance. Mothers work in the kitchen, and many have attended our English classes for adults. Every year when our program concludes, the village turns out to see the sixth graders graduate, the folk dances performed by each grade, and to enjoy the shared celebratory cakes.

When we have asked some of our graduates about what it was like to grow up in Los Ricos, we hear again and again about the positives. They talk of riding horses, swimming in the river, working with the family in the fields, and close friendships. The phrase heard most often is "I would not have wanted to grow up anywhere else." These graduates have a strong sense of who they are and where they are from—it's a priceless heritage passed down through the generations.

CHAPTER 12

Sharing Stories from Los Ricos

THE KINDER

Located up the hill from Naciones Unidas with its own fence, building, and school bureaucracy, the Los Ricos kinder (ages three to five) is physically separate from the elementary school but they are also fed by Feed the Hungry. On a cold winter day in January 2005, no one was there as the wind whistled through it. Without windowpanes or a door, it was like a shell. Mothers were rightly reluctant to leave their tiny children in the cold building. Even if they had, there was little furniture, just a couple of small desks stacked in a corner. As the years went on, the school district started paying more attention to the kinder classroom and eventually put in a door, windowpanes, desks, a playground, and even toilets. A carload of our volunteers would show up every Wednesday in the winter to take on the roomful of energetic children.

The first vehicle rolls out of a parking lot in San Miguel de Allende at 11:00 a.m. carrying five volunteer kindergarten teachers. We arrive a while later at *Escuela* Naciones Unidas.

The kinders are energetic and enthusiastic, and after an hour or so of "Hokey Pokey," "Wheels on the Bus," and colors and numbers with the three- to five-year-old children, the other five vehicles carrying the rest of the volunteers pull in—we hope!

We are never quite sure the SUVs which carry the volunteers will make it up the steep, rutted hill to the school. Some cars have to park at the nearby monastery, the volunteers shuttled over in cars with higher clearance. One year, when the Río Laja was flooded, we all walked across the swinging bridge from the monastery. Lucha, the dauntless director, occasionally has children out on the road hauling rocks to fill in the potholes so the intrepid drivers can make it up the hill.

The English lessons then begin for the first six grades and a handful of adults who want to learn English to help their kids with their homework or better their own chances for employment. The adults range in age from seventeen to forty-five and, as Lucha often says, each one has a story that could fill a book! And, speaking of books, each class gets to go to the school library and take out a book, a high point of the day. After class, the mothers feed us a delicious comida, their way of thanking us for our time with their children.

Then the junior high and high school students arrive, hot and tired after walking from their schools in Atotonilco, we tutor them in English to supplement their lessons at school, and by the time we head home to San Miguel around 4:00, we are hot and tired ourselves.

We are grateful to the community of Los Ricos for welcoming us into their lives, entrusting us with their beautiful children, and sharing a special day with them during our winter teaching program. They have given us back as much if not more than anything we have given to them.

WE TEACH, WE LEARN

For the first through sixth grades, we had started with the basics—greetings, colors, numbers, directions, simple instructions, simple vocabulary beginning with the familiar items found in each classroom, such as desk, table, whiteboard, markers, paper, pencil, etc. We made worksheets with pictures and fill-in-the-blanks. These were a novelty for students as there are no copy machines in rural schools. Students showed no hesitancy to participate in the icebreaker songs to start the class. Hands eagerly raised to step to the front of the class and be the leader of the "Hokey Pokey." We were moving right along. Once the secundaria and prepa students started coming back from Atotonilco for afternoon tutoring, teachers at first wanted a text to lean on. A popular United States book was purchased with a grant from the Unitarian Fellowship of San Miguel. Students were pleased to have a book and for the first couple of years, it gave teachers some security that they were covering the basics. Teachers could pick and choose the lessons based on appropriateness. Soon it became clear that the books were intended to orient an immigrant to United States culture. So much was not applicable to rural Mexico. Teaching vocabulary for a building that included basements, attics, and traditional wooden construction seemed a chapter to skip, as were many more.

Soon teachers began to make their own assessments and observations as to what students knew and what they needed to know. A couple of seventh- and eighth-grade teachers began to build lessons based on geography. Where is Los Ricos in the world? The cardinal directions, map-reading skills, and how to give directions were the focus of lessons.

In the fifth and sixth grade, it was decided to build the curriculum based on a relevant bilingual book, incorporating reading, writing, speaking, and listening with an emphasis on critical thinking skills. Books chosen were those available in the Learning Center.

We asked students to write about what they know as a way to boost their confidence. Journals and journal writing were introduced as an important part of the lesson, drawing on their knowledge about living in the campo. When they could write and share with others, it was a big confidence booster and motivator toward the goal of using observation, thought, and reflection to form opinions or to write a story. It also improved fluency and vocabulary. All journal writing was in Spanish. This type of open-ended writing seemed new to the students. It didn't happen right away, but over time as classmates wrote and shared their writing, others joined in responding enthusiastically. Teachers modeled by writing and sharing their own journal entries. It always helped to have one fluent Spanish-speaking teacher in the class to help us translate our writings. Students learned more about their teachers, and teachers learned more about their students, to everyone's benefit. Students also recognized that we were struggling to learn Spanish as they struggled to learn English.

THE ADULT CLASS: PAINT BUCKETS TO THE COMEDOR

My first memory of the adult class was after the afternoon tutoring was in full swing, and the kids were looking to their mothers for help. A few women were working as housekeepers in town, and several had jobs at nearby Los Labradores across the main highway as housekeepers or skilled aides in their nursing facility. Many had family in the US, and some had spent time there themselves, but few had much English. The women asked for a class so they could help their kids or make themselves more marketable for jobs in town.

Our first "classroom" wasn't at the school; instead, it was at the bottom of the hill below the schoolyard in the home of Adriana, one of the adult students, since we hadn't yet built the comedor at the school. Both teachers and students sat on empty paint buckets. Dogs wandered through, and frequently a mom or two would bring their infants and nurse them while juggling notebooks and trying to balance on the buckets on the dirt floor.

Four of us taught Adriana, Norma, José Manuel (a former student), and a few others. A dramatic class was when José Manuel showed up late to class with bleeding gums, having just had several teeth extracted by a dentist in the Patronato Pro Niños dental van parked in the school's patio.

As always, there were families that did not get along with other families. Long-standing grudges caused some students not to attend class in Adriana's home. Likewise, a year later after the comedor was built, some of those original families chose not to attend when we moved back to the school, and we will never know the family feuds or underlying misunderstandings. Happily, several found employment, but their schedules did not allow them to attend classes. The comedor, built as a place for children to eat but used for everything else, was a great classroom!

Once the mothers started making lunch for the volunteer teachers, they had to pass right through the comedor/English class with their food to get to the kitchen. (Their mole was so good that I still dream of it.) We often would invite these women to stay for class, but most were too shy.

We tried to gear the class to whatever was pressing each week: weather, food, time, jobs, and family. The number of students ranged from around six to as few as one or two. Jorge came regularly for years and often brought his smart little daughter Lupita with him. Lucero, Andrea, Alma, and Rosario were regulars. Rosario had been the Feed the Hungry cook along with Alma and was one of our most thoughtful and hardworking students. Reyna, Gloria, and several others added their own points of view. No one was at the same level, and many had to keep their little kids entertained while trying to participate in the class. Horses would appear at the window, dogs still wandered through, and small dramas took place.

The day-to-day struggles of the village often colored the conversation: water issues, strangers with questionable motives buying up land nearby, and always, security. And the community was always hoping to get some support from the county. Invariably, the villagers were expected to contribute money and labor to augment county projects, such as the vado over the Río Laja.

One mighty effort that did not come to fruition was to have the rancho designated an indigenous community. Such a designation would bring many perks, such as classes in Otomí. One of Rosario's daughters was able to go to school in nearby La Cuadrilla, where there were classes in Otomí, and her younger children followed. Although some of the residents had abuelos or tíos who spoke Otomí, the criteria were strict, and the effort was abandoned.

FROM LOS RICOS TO THE BUSINESS WORLD

In 2014, as we met to plan the curriculum, we realized the importance of providing more exposure to what is out there. Students are all too familiar with the difficulty of finding work post-high school. Many have family members or know of villagers who take the risk of going to El Norte. They know the traditional professions and the many years of expensive education required, but they know little of the emerging high-tech automotive and aeronautic plants in Guanajuato and Querétaro and have had little exposure to the technical training required.

Mexiplas, a state-of-the-art automotive plant in the new Querétaro Industrial Park, was managed by Bob Redfern, the CEO and a San Miguel neighbor, who invited us and our students to tour the plant and get a taste of the new México. We jumped at the opportunity.

It was a cool, breezy, but sunny morning, as we pulled into the village of Los Ricos. Six students were at our appointed meeting place by the church. All were "lookin' good" for the long-anticipated field trip. A villager, no doubt curious as to why all the cars had suddenly arrived on a Saturday, peeked out of her door, and then retreated. The three teachers who drove their SUVs reviewed their maps and soon we were off.

Soon our drive to Querétaro brought us to the impressive entrance to the Industrial Park with dozens of international companies lining the roads of the complex. The buildings sit on landscaped lots, and the sidewalks and street-lights of this well-maintained park give it an inviting ambiance.

Two young women representing Human Resources warmly welcomed us upon arrival to Mexiplas, leading us to a conference area where they did a PowerPoint presentation on the Mexiplas operation, followed by an industrial engineer who spoke of the specifics of the automotive components made at the company.

After donning safety glasses and being apprised of the plant rules, we began the tour. A second engineer, a young man who was involved in helping set up the workstations with the robotic equipment, explained every aspect of the production. Again, he was an impressive role model for our students. He was enthusiastic about his work and personally related well. We entered the Quality Control Area with its specially controlled climate. There, we saw the gauges and special measuring devices so important to the maintenance of industry standards. In another room, an engineer did careful measurements on a component using a computer. In another area, we saw what happens to the many components deemed substandard. They are put in a machine to be melted down and remade. Nothing is wasted.

The students had the opportunity to see the plant firsthand, but also to meet enthusiastic young professionals who so obviously enjoy what they do. One of our students, Aidé, was particularly struck by the presentation of the Human Resources speaker. As the presentation ended and we left the room, Aidé made the connection. "I could do that!" It was an ah-ha moment for her, one she remembers to this day. She wrote: "When the English teachers provided the opportunity to go to Mexiplas, I was encouraged by seeing women who had good jobs, and I knew that was what I wanted for my life." Aidé was encouraged by this experience to continue studying. After high school, she went to the Universidad de León, graduating with a degree in business administration. It was the same kind of in-person encounter that struck Yessenia in the lawyer's office which helped her decide, "Yes, I can do that. I could be a lawyer."

During the eleventh- and twelfth-grade class the following week, we asked students what they remembered of the presentation by Human Resources. It came through loud and clear: stay in school, get as much education as you can, work hard, get good grades. There are good jobs available if you have the training, especially in math and technical courses. There were lots of steps along the way, but sometimes one field trip is worth a thousand lessons.

Part 5

VOICES OF LOS RICOS DE ABAJO'S HELPING HANDS
—THE VOLUNTEER ENGLISH TEACHERS

CHAPTER 13

The Los Ricos de Abajo Volunteer English Teachers in Their Own Words

DIANNE WALTA HART

D ianne Walta Hart, director of the program and book's co-author: Tom and I live in Corvallis, Oregon, and while on a short sabbatical in the city of Guanajuato in 1992, we visited San Miguel for the first time to visit an old school friend. San Miguel quickly became one of our favorite places. For years afterward, Tom volunteered as a physician at CASA (Center for Adolescents of San Miguel de Allende), while I placed student interns from Oregon universities in appropriate positions, many in San Miguel. In 2000, we retired and then lived there for several months a year.

Los Ricos offered me a window into rural Mexican culture. I had studied and taught Latin American culture, but I had always wondered where Mexicans went when they stepped off the highway onto an undesignated path or exited a bus in a rural area. Where did they go? What was their life like there? Relying on my academic research background in oral history at Oregon State University (focusing on Nicaragua and undocumented immigrants in Los Angeles) and then writing articles about the kitchen cooks for Feed the Hungry gave me the first tiny insight into rural lives.

The Los Ricos English program became a gift of what all the textbooks or classes in the world cannot teach: shared friendships across many cultures, love, tears, puzzlement, organizational challenges, disappointments, shock, pride, difficult decisions, plans made and unmade, lunches made by the mothers, and mostly becoming part of the lives of people who step off that bus and walk into what had previously been unknown.

Another unexpected gift was the community that developed among the teachers. My husband and I, like many of the volunteers, spent our lives surrounded by people with similar professional interests. Now we had, without realizing it ahead of time, become part of another community of Los Ricos teachers who came from all parts of the world, all professions, all backgrounds, and all religions. We all loved children, whether we had our own or not, and were accepting of the ambiguities that come with living in another culture and country. That brought us together. That and a few jokes about our car meeting the Coke bottle truck on a narrow hilly Los Ricos road with no way to back up or get out of the way.

CAROLYN WELLS SIMSARIAN

Carolyn Wells Simsarian, teacher, recruiter, and book's co-author: We moved to San Miguel de Allende in 2010. John retired as an administrator for mental health in state government and I retired after a career teaching high school English. Bill and Pam Amidon suggested we teach at a school in the campo. Like Dianne, we were curious about the people who lived in the remote villages surrounding San Miguel.

I joined the National Teacher Corps in 1966, the Corps' inaugural year, and following training was assigned to a school in inner-city Detroit, Michigan. We lived in Detroit while John was pursuing a master's degree in social work, and I received a master's in education. We enjoyed Detroit, its people and its diversity. These were turbulent, yet exciting times; positive social change was happening!

The Teacher Corps encouraged connection and, above all, finding a way to engage students in their own learning through innovative teaching techniques. An important premise of our teacher corps team was, if a student failed, the teacher had in effect failed to reach that student. That precept stayed with me throughout my teaching career.

We really had no contact or knowledge of rural life in Central Mexico before joining the project. Moving to Mexico felt like an adventure. We were open and eager to learn all we could about the country and the Mexican people. Mexico welcomed us, and we were eager to give back, to contribute.

The primary school at Los Ricos at first seemed basic in terms of its physical structure and was lacking supplies and equipment. Yet, here were happy and smiling kids running out to greet us. The school, situated on a windy hilltop, was bathed in sunshine as bright as the children's smiles. In the distance lay a beautiful vista of fields and mountains. For all that may be lacking, there was the warmth of the welcome and the natural setting to make up for it.

From that welcome, we expected this was going to be fun, it would be challenging, and we were going to learn a lot. We were hopeful that the students would learn as well. We didn't have everything figured out at once. There is an expression in Mexico "poco a poco," which means "a little at a time." In this way, the project grew as we tried to respond to the needs of the students.

As we met at the end of the season to discuss what went well, what needed improvement, and how to go about achieving our goals, it felt as if we were doing something significant. When our first students graduated from high school and then from a university, there was a tremendous feeling of satisfaction and pride in their accomplishments. The other volunteers were open to trying new approaches. Our director would present our ideas to the principal for approval and then we had the freedom to discover teaching strategies that worked.

We've seen students learn, grow, and change over time. We've seen them set goals and accomplish them. It is a great feeling to hear returning students, poised and confident, inspire their audience as they describe their journey, its challenges and rewards, and how important it is to stay in school and get an education. Younger students learn from these role models, taking it all in.

The voices of students in this book are representative of all the students in Los Ricos. The community has given its best by providing for the school and supporting it. The mothers of the village have made us feel welcome, fed us, and celebrated the achievements of their children with us. The connection we feel to the school, the children, and the people of Los Ricos gives us hope for the future.

JACKIE DONNELLY

Jackie Donnelly, one of the first teachers and co-director of the second year: My first contact with Los Ricos came after my initial meeting with the president of Feed the Hungry who was aware of my background in world language teaching methods and approached me to start an English program in a small rural school, Los Ricos, outside of San Miguel. Chad Payne, a talented man with great computer skills, joined the team. Chad was on a sabbatical from Price Waterhouse at the time. Our challenge was to write a program that would be appropriate for the various ages and learning levels. I structured the lessons around the Total Physical Response method where the students learned the language through movement. We met weekly to create the lessons, honing them as we went along. The entire school would assemble in the playground, lined up according to classes. We began with the social formalities of "Hello" and "How are you," and then proceeded en masse to teach the students vocabulary, such as body parts, through the game "Simon Says" and playful pantomimes to teach vocabulary. The students then went to their classrooms to continue the lessons with the volunteer teachers. I remember my class well, all were bright, eager, and so affectionate.

PAM AMIDON

Pam Amidon, an early volunteer and recruiter: My husband, Bill, and I discovered San Miguel de Allende in 2008. It was love at first sight for us. Through an email introduction, we met John and Carolyn Simsarian, who knew people in our Boston condo.

During that time, I met Dianne Hart through a post she had made on San Miguel's Civil List explaining her need to find people in San Miguel who had elementary teaching experience and could help with a project at Los Ricos, a tiny village outside San Miguel.

Having retired recently as a second-grade teacher, I immediately contacted her. After many emails back and forth, I decided that this was a wonderful opportunity to get involved in something new and exciting.

In the beginning, I wrote the curriculum, which I loved doing as I had always wanted to get into curriculum work, but I never imagined it would be in Mexico. I will never forget the first day Rex Morgan and I had the first- and second-grade classroom. I had learned silencio and siéntate. Rex had about ten more words in Spanish than I had. It was truly crazy, but we survived. At this time Bill was not interested in teaching and had nothing to do with Los Ricos. He was still busy with the house and yard. But eventually, Bill signed on as we needed drivers, and we had a big SUV to make it through rivers and mud. He finally agreed to drive and help Jan Friedman in her class. Then he was hooked.

My memories are of hard work, often frustrating, and lots of laughs. Head, shoulders, knees, and toes led by the late Lois Weiss will always be in my head as we sang it gustily at the end of every class. After many years of driving out to Los Ricos, I remember Bill saying loudly, "I will never do this again. My car is getting ruined." But of course, he did.

Bill and I brought lots of people into teaching there as we loved it, and our love was contagious. The whole group became friendly and saw each other often for dinner or parties. The group is still social and committed to this little hamlet, and as I reflect on my time in San Miguel, I can really say that it was life-enhancing. What luck to have the opportunity to work with such a great group led by Dianne, Lucha, and all the kids!

SUZANNE BACON

Suzanne Bacon, chief of just about everything: I am Suzanne Bacon, born in Pennsylvania and brought up in New Jersey, but now identify with Boston and New England more than any other place in the United States. I vacationed in San Miguel in 1992 and now have been in San Miguel more than in Boston. I retired from a career in information technology and have seen it all, from the room-sized Univac III to the smartwatch that recently asked me, while I was face down on a tope on Calzada de la Aurora, if I had really "fallen and needed help?"

My first introduction to Feed the Hungry and, in turn, Los Ricos de Abajo happened in 2013 when the Amidons attended a committee at Old South Church in Boston and made a pitch for us to support Feed the Hungry, and their plea gave me the opportunity to visit Los Ricos.

Not only did I participate in 2015, but I was asked to be the lead teacher in kinder, which I reluctantly accepted. Not exactly a good talent match, but I was game. I had had no teaching experience, no children or grandchildren, nor any education or training in this area. I didn't even know the songs!! All I had ever disciplined or taught were dogs. Oh, and did I mention that my Spanish is pretty bad! It didn't take too long for me to gravitate to what I do best, which is planning and organizing. I would make a plan and then turn it over to the other volunteers who were better Spanish speakers, and more comfortable with these squirmy, adorable three- to five-year-old children. I remember thinking at the end of our program that year that these youngsters knew at least one word in English— "kneesandtoes." On the final day, we were entertained with a combination of traditional Mexican folk dancing and the occasional hip-hop number. I was totally enchanted with this beautiful little village, the children, and the mothers. The children's capacity for eating cake was unparalleled and the generosity of the mothers, who prepared a feast for us, was over the top.

The second year, I was much better prepared and gave each assistant a bag of tricks and off we went. If the board book wasn't appealing to them, we went on to dice and counting. If that didn't work, we colored and practiced our colors, which invariably turned into a shouting match … who could say "purple" the loudest? When all else failed, we had songs. We even used props for "Wheels on the Bus." It was then that I noticed subtle differences between Mexican and American children. The Mexicans showed no possessiveness and little competition. Sharing was second nature to these children.

Of course, there was always the day that was windy or some holiday or other when there was no controlling the fifteen to twenty youngsters even with five adults in the room. One time, John Simsarian took the concept of meeting students at their level to a whole new low—he's six feet six and crawled under the table with a small group of four-year-old children.

I have always been fascinated with which lessons worked and which did not. One class of eighth graders where I assisted Gary Davidson was a total surprise to me. He brought in hammers and drills, and we had them do a small construction project. I was appalled. What if they hit their fingers or drilled holes in their hands?! These typically bored teenagers, mostly girls, became totally engaged and took pride in their little projects, respected their tools, and caused no harm. I was shocked.

One year, I endeared myself to a small group of ninth-grade girls by making fun of my Spanish and showing how learning another language is difficult—for them and for me. We had some good laughs over the love of music we shared. Being silly with them about their music choices, what they liked to do in their free time, and dancing brought me back to those years as a teenager.

Dianne and John enlisted me to take on staffing responsibilities, which is absolutely the right job for me! I was particularly pleased the year we introduced bilingual yoga and soccer. It was then that I realized that thinking of this program as teaching English was not what we are all about. For one thing, we don't spend that much time with the students over the course of a season. What we are really accomplishing is exposing them to the potential of education. In the younger groups, it is about having fun and being creative. It is about introducing choices and critical-thinking skills. It is about books and hopefully the joy of reading. For a few, it is exposing them to the choices they may have if they stay in school. It is about introducing the idea of a career to them and helping them to make choices.

As I reflect on this program, I learn more each week about another culture, another age group, and skills I have not used in the past. In no small part, it gives me the opportunity to know a community of fellow volunteers in other than a purely social setting. We problem-solve together. We get to know each other's strengths and weaknesses. We totally respect one another and the community we have grown to love. We have built and continue to build a program that enhances the lives of these children and improves understanding between two worlds. I am enriched.

ALICE VERHOEVEN

Alice Verhoeven, head librarian and transportation coordinator: I was born and raised in New Jersey. A job with a feminine hygiene company led to an interest in health education. In 1971, I moved to San Francisco for graduate study in community health and started volunteering as a health counselor in the teen health center at Planned Parenthood. That was the start of a fifty-three-year career in women's health (forty years with Planned Parenthood and thirteen years with a community hospital system in Cambridge, Massachusetts). In 1977, my East Coast roots started tugging and I moved to the Boston area where I have lived ever since. I consider myself a New Englander now, but part of me will always be a "Jersey girl."

I first visited San Miguel in 2009 to check it out as a retirement location, and since then I've spent every winter and usually sometime in the fall in San Miguel as well.

The Amidons introduced me to Los Ricos in one of my early visits to San Miguel. In those days, we met at Dianne and Tom Hart's house, and all piled into cars. Pam told me about the school and the students, but not about the road. I was aghast once we turned off the paved road and started along the rutted dirt road. When we came to the river, I thought I was going to lose it. I wondered "how and why do these people do this every week?" When we finally arrived at the school and the kids rushed to their regular teachers with hugs and big smiles, I knew why.

That first day, I assisted in the first and second grades. Pam had a lesson on numbers, and I'll never forget those big brown eyes of one boy as he stared at me and tried so hard to repeat the numbers. I was hooked. Each time I visited San Miguel, I went out to Los Ricos and assisted in various grades and the library, which was started by Pam Mosco and Jan Friedman. The library was always my favorite because you got to see all the kids. Watching them rush to get (and sometimes fight over) their favorite books—princesses for the girls, and cars, trucks, dinosaurs, and reptiles for the boys—confirmed that kids are pretty much the same all over. I've loved seeing the changes (some good, others not so much) in the children as the years went by.

Since retiring in late 2013, I've signed on full-time to Los Ricos. I've planted seeds with third graders, held my breath in the fourth grade with hammers and nails for the lesson, caught the giggles from a devilish group of seventh-grade boys during my "let's make a pizza" lesson, and learned a big lesson about what not to do when bringing food to the classroom: make sure you bring enough of the *same* fruit to avoid the melee that broke out over the pineapple after my fruit lesson in fourth grade. Duh, what was I thinking?

In 2017, I took on two new roles: managing the library and scheduling transportation. The library has been a joy and was always my favorite place. It's been fun experimenting with different ways to organize the books, by trying different rotations for class levels, getting classroom teachers more involved as well as trying to get secundaria students to take out books. Peppa Pig and Coco have been recent favorites and, of course, we still have to break up the occasional fights over princess and shark books.

Transportation, on the other hand, has been a challenge. Former self-dubbed "Commish" Rex Morgan cajoled me into taking this on, assuring me "there's nothing to it." Ha, I should have checked with Sam Zimmerman who did the job before Rex. Each week, it's a juggling act to match the drivers with the number of teachers. There are the eleventh-hour texts/calls from drivers who cancel with car trouble or illness, then the scramble to find backup drivers. Our antennae are always up looking for new volunteer drivers with SUVs.

Every fall, my thoughts turn to river-water levels and road conditions. Reports from the Zimmermans, Tom Knapp, and Dianne's village contacts help us understand what we'll face in January. Finally, 2020 saw major and permanent improvements. Los Ricos families and the county put their muscles to work building a vado across the river.

I am grateful to the Los Ricos community and this program for all I have learned about Mexican families and their culture of sharing and resilience. Equally valuable to me are the friends and connections I've made through the volunteer network of Los Ricos and Feed the Hungry. I can't imagine life in San Miguel without it.

BOB BOWERS

Bob Bowers, chief kid magnet, writes: Why am I a kid magnet? First off, I'd say, who knows? We all know people with special attractions. For instance, the number of times visiting households with cats I've heard people say to my partner David, "I'm amazed Fluffy is doing that; he's really shy around people" as their shy/anti-social cat twined around his ankles and considered a cuddle in his lap. It's a natural gift he's got. I would guess if I had to put an analysis to it, I'm a kid magnet because I really like them, find them interesting, enjoy their company, and encourage them to interact with me. That interaction feeds me as much as it does them and maybe they can sense that.

When I was teaching in Chicago, I became the in-school advisor for a scholarship group of kids, almost exclusively Latino, who came from good but poor families, which meant their high school experiences would have been in some of the worst schools in Chicago. They received full scholarships from a church group, which also encouraged them to study hard, keep off the streets by participating in activities in the center, and stay in school. They had a remarkable success rate with retention and graduations. Over the years, I became the mentor or benevolent/stern uncle figure. I kept track of their grades, attendance, behavior, and extracurricular activities as well as interacting with and helping with their personal life issues. (For example, I know about twenty-three ways to comfort someone when his girlfriend has dumped him!) In 2002, the leader of the group who had been to San Miguel several times said to me, "These kids think they're poor; I want to show them what poor really looks like. Would you like to go along?" He suggested an eighteen-day mission trip to San Miguel de Allende, coordinated with the local Baptist Church, with the kids staying in town but going out daily into the campo to work in the poorer communities. We didn't get to Los Ricos de Abajo, but I did work most of my time nearby in La Petaca. It was the first time I'd ever done anything like that, and I fell in love with the idea, the work, and the place. After that, I began vacationing in San Miguel and, a few years later, when the time to retire arrived, I decided to reverse my life so that I lived in San Miguel de Allende and vacationed in Chicago! I have now lived for over ten years in a house that is exactly one block from the rooming house used during my first visit, that to me feels like a puzzle piece that's fallen exactly into place.

It was always firmly in my mind to find ways to volunteer within the community as soon as I got here. I interviewed to work with one program teaching English but quickly realized that I wasn't going to be able to meet their needs. That night, feeling discouraged, I had dinner in El Rinconcito Restaurant on Refugio Norte and struck up a conversation with fellow South Dakotans Tom and Dianne Hart. Dianne just happened to have a suggestion for a work activity that might be more my speed. I've learned that Dianne often has good suggestions, and this was certainly one of her better ones! During my first hour on the job site, before classes had even started, I found myself sitting on the ground, my whiteboard and markers out, interacting with little kids. Their English was nonexistent, and my Spanish was not much better at that point, but we communicated, learned some color names, and had fun.

My time with the program has been and continues to be some of the most rewarding, fulfilling, and downright fun experiences of my life. Once, early in the years I lived here, a woman at a party asked me, "What do you do?" Everybody there was some sort of artist, writer, or something important.

I smiled at her and said, "I'm a nose-wiper." It's true; I am a nose-wiper (sometimes literally at Los Ricos!). That, to me, means a caregiver. I give them what they need—knowledge first and foremost, support, affection, companionship, aid, and comfort when that's needed. It's what keeps me centered and gives me immense satisfaction, and, yes, I consider that every bit as important as a poet being able to write a good poem.

DOUG LORD

Doug Lord, chief tuition funds distributor, mentor, and Saturday teacher: I am Douglas Lord and lived in San Miguel de Allende for twenty years. My wife Brianne and I came in 2003 from San Francisco to retire. Before that I was a trial lawyer for thirty-seven years, the first twenty years representing working-class people in Richmond. For the last seventeen years, I concentrated on suing insurance companies for wrongfully denying claims. Throughout this time, I was involved in community activities and Democratic politics, and served as a delegate at the 1968 Democratic Convention in Chicago.

When we first came to San Miguel, I volunteered with the San Miguel School of English, where I taught English to Mexican adults for about a year. They ranged from maids and waiters to architects, lawyers, and doctors. During that time, I also met a man who told me he knew the principal of an elementary school out in the country who said that if you wanted to do something significant here, you could actually save lives by teaching English to kids out in the campo. Then my daughter, who lives in Oregon, showed me an article by an Oregon State University teacher named Dianne Hart. It was about starting up an English-speaking program in a small rancho outside of Atotonilco. I contacted Dianne, went to a couple of meetings, and started teaching elementary school kids at Los Ricos de Abajo. I had no contact with or knowledge of people who live in the countryside of Central Mexico before the Los Ricos project and it was an opportunity to learn something about Mexican culture.

My first impression of the Los Ricos school was that of surprise at how basic, remote, and kind of desolate it was. I remember wondering why this place of only about three hundred people would've originally been settled. It didn't have particularly good arable land to farm, so the inhabitants had to travel a bit to raise the typical crop of corn and beans. But it is a tight community where most adults and children share a good relationship. Some extended families have their own separate compounds with three or four houses built on ejido property. Each family builds their own house, sometimes with money sent from the United States, where the father or grandfather has been working.

I kept teaching and driving out to the school every season because I like the Los Ricos folks a lot and made many good relationships. I also made many good friends with the teachers I met through the program. At the Los Ricos graduation festival every year the students put on a show, and in one of the first years, the kids all dressed up in Ballet Folklórico costumes and did traditional Mexican dances. Another year, the kids performed as part of a fundraiser for Feed the Hungry at the Rosewood Hotel. This time the girls wore white dresses, swooping onto the dance floor to perform a more European dance. On another special occasion, we teachers were all invited to a fiesta with the family of one of our best students, Maritza. She showed us around the house, the vegetable garden, and the little pigs that they had in an enclosure. The house was nestled in a group of houses that belong to their extended family, with grandparents, uncles, aunts, and cousins in daily interaction. We were also invited to graduations; the first was a special one where Maritza and her friend Yessenia put together a reception after the usual church service. The girls raised the money themselves for the mariachi band and a nice outdoor lunch. All the relatives were there; it was a special event for the families since, for many, it was their first high school graduation.

One year, veteran teacher Bob Bowers and I decided that we wanted to spend time with the students all year round, not just during the January through March season, so we started having Saturday English classes at my house in San Miguel, which was conveniently located near the bus stop for our Los Ricos kids. So the classes started, and at one point we were teaching four different levels of classes, including one for adults from Los Ricos.

Since 2014, I have been the scholarship cashier, giving out monthly stipends for tuition and other essentials to the students who have enrolled in the various universities in the area. The money comes from the generous donations of Michael Chadwick, our teachers, and other donors. The students come to the house, pick up the money, and we have a nice chat about what they have been doing. I have been able to follow their careers.

JOHN SIMSARIAN

John Simsarian, teacher and recruiter: Our first visit to San Miguel was in 2005 when we came during Carolyn's spring break from teaching. I retired in 2006 following my career as an administrator for mental health and substance abuse programs in state government. On a return visit in 2008, we went to Los

Ricos having been recruited by the Amidons. The program was part of our decision to buy a house and move here in 2009. We've been involved with the program ever since. I've always said that visiting the school and interacting with the kids made Wednesday the highlight of my week.

I had little knowledge of rural life in Mexico. The idea of being able to meet the inhabitants of this remote village, see village life while learning more about Mexico, was appealing. My first and no less important role in the program was as a driver, conveying volunteers out to the school. There was always lively chatter in anticipation of seeing the kids, as well as great sharing of stories on the return. Navigating the dirt roads, fording the river, and at last reaching the village increased its sense of isolation. I was struck by the lack of resources at the school, but at the same time appreciated the beauty of the school's bucolic setting on the hill. I anticipated meeting friendly people. My expectations were met despite my lack of Spanish. People were accepting and communicative.

I started out as a teacher's assistant in the primary grades. As the program grew, I worked with the adults and later the kindergarten as those programs were added. I also assisted with the fifth and sixth grades. Gradually, I took on some of the support services, such as distributing textbooks, tallying attendance, recruiting, and assigning volunteers. Volunteers were flexible, and always willing to fill in where needed.

The rewards were many. I got to know Alma in the adult program and enjoyed checking in with her in the kitchen where, as the cook, she was at the heart of the lunch program. The adult class began at the request of parents who saw their ability to speak English as a way to increase employment opportunities. Many of these eager adult students had not had much opportunity to attend school themselves.

In the kinder program, I saw children progress. Many of these three- to five-year-olds were just learning Spanish. Here we were holding up pictures of a "COW." "No," they rightfully insisted, "es una VACA!"

THE ZIMMERMANS

Bob and Nancy (Sam) Zimmerman, handyman and assistant librarian: We arrived in San Miguel in January 2008 for the winter. We had never been to San Miguel, but we had been to several places throughout Mexico. Bob is a retired forensic accountant, and I (Sam) am a retired banker and former teacher. Since 2011, we have lived in San Miguel full-time and returned to the United States only once.

One evening in January 2008, we were having dinner at El Rinconcito in Colonia San Antonio. Another couple was sitting next to us and before we knew it, Dianne and Tom Hart asked if we wanted to go to a community called Los Ricos de Abajo to teach English. I, being a former teacher, immediately jumped at the opportunity. Bob was wondering what he was going to do but was willing to go along for the ride and adventure. (He didn't have to wonder for long.) I was helping in the fifth- and sixth-grade classroom and Bob found a lot of little maintenance projects to keep him busy. Soon, I was the lead teacher and developed a variety of programs, including teaching the students about gardening and healthy eating. I also organized all the transportation for about twenty-five volunteers. Later I worked in the library where I organized all the check-ins and check-outs and taught English on Saturdays to some of the high school students.

Bob has done a lot of projects at Los Ricos. He removed rocks from the toilets, took away stones on the *tinaco* valve, replaced many broken windows, planted geraniums in the front of the school, and replaced the shotgun fuse in the back corner of the schoolyard for a real circuit breaker. Bob was busy from the time he arrived until he left. On each visit, he checked in with Lucha, other teachers, and the cooks to see what was needed, and each week he left with a new list of items to be repaired the following week.

He even had an adventure with a frog when he and another teacher went to the girls' bathroom to repair a broken lid. Bob looked in the back of the water tank and saw a frog. Not wanting to hurt the frog, he scooped it up gently with his hand. Suddenly, the frog jumped and landed in the toilet bowl. This toilet bowl hadn't been cleaned in a while, leaving Bob and the teacher trying to figure out what to do. While they pondered the situation, a small female student behind them reached over and flushed the toilet ... Bye-Bye, Froggie.

We have seen many of the students on the streets of San Miguel. It warms our hearts every time they come up to say hello and introduce us to their parents. Now some of the students we first met in 2008 are young adults, some have completed university, some are married, and some have young children of their own. It is also a delight when we run into Lucha.

MORE TEACHERS CHIME IN

Diana Couper: I am a retired English as a Second Language teacher and spent my whole career teaching in the New York City public school system. I worked in Brooklyn in one of the poorest, roughest, and most crime-ridden districts in New York City.

I still live in Brooklyn, but when I was about to retire in 2011, I revisited San Miguel de Allende, a place where I had spent the summer of 1982, and bought a home. During the first month, I wandered over to the Aldea Hotel to visit the Unitarian Fellowship. There I met and chatted with Carolyn Simsarian. She mentioned the Los Ricos program or maybe I told her that I was a retired ESL teacher. Either way, I was recruited and became a happy volunteer.

I had no experience of life in rural Mexico. I had some idea of life in Central America and the Caribbean from my immigrant students who were mostly from poor families and from rural communities. I observed that in some ways Los Ricos is like my Brooklyn community. There are families that are highly functional even with few resources and others that are dysfunctional with domestic violence. Strong women are present and active in the school to improve their kids' lives.

Based on my Brooklyn experience, I expected that students living in poverty with few opportunities would be angry and/or depressed, would act out in the classroom, and have little respect for teachers who didn't carry a big stick. To my surprise, in Los Ricos, there is little to no violence in the school and few disciplinary problems in the classroom, and students are friendly and respectful to the volunteers. That is not to say that there are no angry and depressed students in Los Ricos. But somehow those students are not constantly disrupting the classrooms.

I volunteered for about five years at Los Ricos then took a break. The Los Ricos experience emboldened me to apply for other volunteer positions. I found my way to Thailand where I was assigned to teach English in an elementary school in the mornings and a college for monks in the afternoons. A few years later, I lived and taught in a secondary boarding school for vulnerable girls in Tanzania.

Lyne Daroff: Through my connection at Los Ricos and Feed the Hungry, I was asked if I wanted to help Feed the Hungry's chefs and nutritionists improve their English. That opportunity has given me a special connection and friendship with the staff and Olivia Muñíz Rodríquez, the director of the food program. They have welcomed me into their lives, and my time here in San Miguel has been greatly enriched by their kindness. Teaching at Los Ricos introduced me to the wonderful group of volunteers who put their heart and soul into this special community. It warmed my heart when one of the young girls in our class came and sat with me on the day of the end-of-the-year party. I do hope to see her again.

Jean Degnon: As a gringa in Mexico, I have sometimes found it difficult to form close relationships with locals, especially with those from the ranchos. Our years in Los Ricos have afforded us the rare opportunity to make real friendships with people in that close-knit community. I have had wonderful meals at the homes of students' parents, attended Alma's (she was the Feed the Hungry cook at Los Ricos) traditional dance performances and the memorable wedding of Yessenia and José Iván, celebrated graduations, babies, new jobs, and more. Going on to teach kinder classes for many years, we got to see how it truly "takes a village," as mamas, *tías*, older brothers would come sometimes on horseback to pick up the little ones. I am forever grateful for this opportunity to be a part of the life of this community. They have given me more than I ever gave to them; I learned more from them than they did from me. Gracías!

John Dundas: One of my best-ever memories of Mexico was the family dinner several of us enjoyed one evening at Maritza's home in Los Ricos. It was a view of Mexican life that few gringos have the privilege of seeing and one I'll never forget. She was special and her family was the reason.

Jan Friedman and Pam Mosco: After vacationing in San Miguel and falling in love with the "magical city," Pam Mosco and I, Jan Friedman, decided that this enchanting place would be perfect for a life change and a retirement relocation from New York. Knowing that San Miguel had many expats, we felt comfortable making the move in 2009 with limited memory of high school Spanish, scant knowledge of Mexican culture, and rather a distaste for Mexican fare.

Once settled in our new home, Pam and I joined a Pilates class where Pam Amidon was a member. She talked about being a volunteer teacher at a rural school, Los Ricos de Abajo. Pam and I were excited to hear about this program since we were both former teachers before owning a children's bookstore.

We knew nothing about rural Mexico, so expectations were few. However, after attending a pre-teaching overview meeting and hearing other volunteers speak about their classroom experiences, the dos and don'ts to help you make the most of your teaching time, the Los Ricos community itself, and the route to get there, we began to formulate a better idea about rural Mexico. After driving on a long and treacherous road that students and their school director walked on to get to school, seeing half-built houses without windows and only dirt floors and languishing underfed dogs roaming in areas of litter, rural now became a reality. After seeing such an impoverished community, I wondered if my students would be eager to learn and if they could retain much by receiving only one hour of our teaching a week for three months.

Much to my surprise, the first and second graders came to class with enthusiasm, eagerness, and attentiveness. To my delight, they made a good and often successful attempt to achieve what was asked of them, although it was distracting when a second grader would hide under his desk. The best part of this teaching experience was that the children and I learned from each other. As most of their first or last names were not familiar in English, I sometimes mispronounced them only to be politely corrected, and when I slipped in a Spanish phrase instead of speaking English, I received friendly laughter for my accent. Getting help from and sharing laughter with the late Bill Amidon also added to classroom fun. The experience was enriching and enlightening not only in the classroom, but in the general milieu of the Los Ricos school setting. The school director, Lucha, investigated the reason students were absent, the teachers who worked with limited resources and practiced the old man folk dance and songs with their class, students' mothers who volunteered in the kindergarten class, and those who prepared lunches for the volunteers were all so dedicated to helping the program succeed and lending support to those in need. In essence, the school was like a grounded family in the community.

When Pam and I saw the school library, we thought it could use a lift, so we supplemented it with many age-appropriate Spanish books and metal bookshelves to house them. Pam was the library keeper, and she took great joy in seeing those smiling faces when the children chose their two books each week. They checked them out by saying "My name is" in English. Those little voices always brought Pam a smile. She also enjoyed helping the students find books on subjects that were of interest to them.

Both Pam and I are so grateful that we had the opportunity to be part of the Los Ricos program. We sadly left the program to move back to the States in 2014 as we missed our families. We will always treasure the children's smiling faces, contagious giggles, and drawings. The children proudly showed us their new shoes and sparkly dresses. And of course, the end of the year show, the three sheet cakes representing Mexico, USA, and Canada, and Tom Hart saying, "Would you like a cookie?"

Ron Kearns: How does one begin to list simple pleasures that can be so rare… or perhaps rarely noticed these days? It's easy to measure our capacity for giving. We may do it most days. Yet to be conscious of what's received each day leads us to gratitude. And remembering the gifts of children brings us to innocence.

Anytime the subject of volunteering at Los Ricos comes up in a conversation, I'll always include how I was introduced to that idea: I was at a Sunday afternoon gathering at a friend's house. I was planning to spend more time in

San Miguel de Allende that year. On the patio I found myself speaking with John Simsarian and telling him of my plans. He replied by telling me of his involvement at Los Ricos. He went on to describe his Wednesdays there as his most fun day and the highlight of his week. Being a kid lover, I could imagine what he said being true and replied, "I would love to do something like that!" Then John broke the news that might break the bubble that I was imagining I would discover in my initial experience of teaching kinders English. He said, "Actually, Ron, it's not as simple as just teaching English. There's an element more like crowd control!" We laughed, I got it, and he wasn't kidding … but it was fun and rewarding on all counts.

Our talk taught me an early lesson, that despite good intentions of offering our time and gifts, we were there to learn as well, have fun, and receive the many gifts a small community in the campo has to offer. To mention a few: the meaning of the word "adorable" to describe the eyes of a four-year-old looking into mine as I demonstrated cutting with scissors. I looked down and noticed she was not paying any attention to what I was showing her. Instead, her eyes were staring intently into mine. Or, how we would be greeted by the children first thing in the morning. Pulling up in our car below the school and its gate, we would be met with smiling faces and open palms waving through the fence every week. Entering the gate, we were then met with arms around our legs, happy faces looking up waiting for hugs or at least a good pat on the head. And then there was the sense of adventure and camaraderie we shared as a group of … shall I say elderly gringos? Who met early Wednesday mornings to share the ride into a country village, over dusty dirt roads, and even fording a stream bed. We enjoyed what we were up to and each other!

Kristen Timothy Lankester: My memorable moments were when my Los Ricos students showed real interest in reading books. One of my seventh-grade girls asked for a copy of *The Diary of Anne Frank* to take home to read. I was delighted. Two of my seventh-grade girls were selected to attend the San Miguel Writers' Conference. I was so proud of them and happy for them to have the opportunity to see more of the world. I believe that teaching English is only part of our mission. The other is to open eyes to the broader world by looking at maps, reading about faraway places, and being exposed to teachers from other parts of the world.

Christie McGue: I live six months of the year in Northern Michigan and six months of the year in San Miguel de Allende. I've been coming to San Miguel since 1996 when I came for a two-week visit with my mother. I fell in love immediately! I returned every year for a week or two until I retired in 2006. That year, my husband Bob came with me, and it was love at first sight for him as well. I had a long career with the federal government in Washington, D.C., but gladly left that behind in 2000 for a slower-paced life in Northern Michigan where I worked for the local land conservancy for six years.

I first heard about the Los Ricos project through John and Carolyn, and even though I had no experience as a teacher and my Spanish was totally inadequate, they encouraged me to give it a chance. From the first visit, I knew it was something I wanted to do.

My first impression of Los Ricos was that it was a place of tremendous joy! The teachers, the students, and the mothers were all so welcoming and happy. I'm embarrassed now to say that I couldn't believe that people who had so little were so joyful, to think that material possessions or lack thereof would determine one's level of happiness. It all seems so trite now, but my experience with children in the United States was much different and much more materialistic. I did not expect that the children would be so excited to see us every week, looking forward to our arrival.

The students and their mothers have kept me enthusiastic. I feel that I get far more from them than I give. While I'm always exhausted at the end of the day, I'm also exhilarated. Now that I've been there for a few years I can see the children maturing and changing. Of course, we also see negative changes, things that happen due to an economic downturn such as a father, uncle, or brother being sent back from the United States, which causes a real monetary hardship on the family.

Two students stand out in my mind, both in the third grade. The first is a boy who acted up in class, constantly picking on others, and especially mean to the girls. We were making valentines for the kids to give to their parents, and most of the boys made cards for their mothers. At the end of the day, when all the children had left and we were cleaning the classroom, I found his valentine on the floor, torn in half. It turns out his mother had left him with his grandmother and had moved to a nearby village with another man. He has since been given special attention by all his instructors and appears to be working through this heartbreaking situation.

The second is a sad little girl. She too lives with her grandparents much of the time. She was quiet and difficult to engage. We have worked hard to give her special attention, but her life circumstances continued to be difficult. During the past school year, a few of us noticed that she was not leaving at the end of the school day, just hanging around. We finally engaged her and found that her grandmother was in San Miguel taking care of another family member who had been hospitalized and would not be back for a few days.

Someone had obviously seen that she had clean clothes and others were seeing that she had food, but she was essentially living on her own. Wow! It gives a whole new meaning to "it takes a village."

Jane McMahon: I live in Connecticut most of the year, but I have been fortunate over the years to visit my Mexican relatives who live in San Miguel. I would visit them during the winter months, and I grew to love life in Mexico. I was looking for an opportunity to do some volunteer work and at the same time perhaps improve my Spanish. When I learned about the Los Ricos program, I was eager to be a part of the effort to teach English in the campo. And what a fulfilling experience it has been! I connected with Alexis Muñoz, and we worked together to improve his English. Alexis has received some financial support along the way from me and has his eye on the prize of receiving a university education. The Los Ricos program provided the launching pad for Alexis, a productive, successful member of society with much to offer.

Rex and Gail Morgan: My husband, Rex, organized a long-dreamed-of trip to the Mexican highlands in 2005. He had always wanted to visit Mexico and thought of retiring there after reading the book *On Mexican Time*. While Rex had studied Spanish in high school, I knew only the vocabulary of street signs I saw growing up in southern California. I had taught computer skills in the '80s, though, to bilingual classes in Berkeley. Many of the students spoke no English, but they picked up the computer skills so quickly and eagerly that I loved working with them.

In 2007, we looked for a house to rent for the winter months and drove our Volkswagen camping van loaded with things we thought we'd need. Driving the Westie (as we called it) through the narrow streets was a nerve-wracking experience, and that's the last time it was our vehicle in Mexico.

Our involvement with Los Ricos began with a luncheon meeting at Jackie Donnelly's to hear about it. Since I was a recently retired teacher of elementary and middle school children, it sounded like a wonderful opportunity to me. Rex was game to try it. That winter we were helpers, following the lead of the more experienced volunteers. Somehow, by the following year, we had been put in charge of the third and fourth graders. Still suffering a great language deficit, we did our best to control the eager, giggly, and sometimes rambunctious students into learning a few words of English through games, songs, and good old-fashioned worksheets. We had the help of other fine people, one who took on the third graders in the windy and wild patio while Rex and I organized the fourth graders into groups that traveled between "learning centers." We got to work with all the students that way, and they seemed to like the various activities, even though the movement and regrouping sometimes seemed chaotic to us. Eventually, Rex was asked to take over the task of organizing carpools to Los Ricos.

As our students grew, so did our program. Along with offering scholarships for the students continuing in secundaria and prepa, we offered continued tutoring. This extended our day as we waited about forty-five minutes after our elementary session ended for the older students to walk back from Atotonilco. The parents of the community decided they should feed us lunch while we waited. Despite our protests, they went ahead, and each week treated us to a luncheon of traditional foods. This was another chance to get to know our fellow volunteers and the mothers of Los Ricos. The older students trickled in, and Dr. Tom welcomed them with cookies and juice, insisting that they respond in proper English when he asked, "Would you like a cookie?" and "Would you like some juice?" We did our best to help them with English, which they were now studying in school. We came to discover that, although English was a mandatory subject in their school, the teachers had limited English themselves, especially when it came to pronunciation.

Each year we enjoyed beginning the year with a dinner at El Rinconcito with all the volunteers. The year ended with a celebration put on by the community with dancing and singing performances. As we get older, we chuckle to think we are part of Los Viejitos.

Julie Preis: I live in Maryland and in San Miguel in the winter and another month or two in the summer. I worked in early childhood education for a long time, then another long time in programs serving senior citizens, then after I retired, I started volunteering with kids. I heard about the program through my sister-in-law who had lived in San Miguel and was friends with Jan Friedman and Pam Mosco who started the library at Los Ricos. I eventually decided to investigate being a volunteer tutor. I got John Simsarian's name, contacted him in December 2015, and was assigned to teach in the 2016 session.

My job was to lead the third grade and co-lead the eighth grade, but I didn't know what to expect. Before classes started, I met with the other eighth-grade lead teacher. Not the meeting I'd hoped for! She complained about how much work was expected of the lead teachers and declared the class would follow the online app Duolingo. Fortunately, the other volunteer teachers were more flexible, and we ended up working in small groups using a combination of Duolingo (when the internet was working) and our own activities. Sam Zimmerman was especially helpful to me and gave me some excellent pointers.

In the third grade that first year, I was fortunate to teach with Chad Payne, a volunteer who had been with the program since the beginning. He was happy to step back and follow my sometimes-weird lesson plans, rescuing me when I needed it. Chad was fluent in Spanish and already much loved by the kids, which really helped me to gain confidence and to be accepted. Before I started at Los Ricos, someone told me that the kids were shy, but those third graders put that notion to rest quickly.

I stayed with the project because I love the kids, have found kindred spirits among the volunteers, and have improved my teaching and Spanish skills enough to think I can contribute. I still have a lot to learn about the people and the community, about teaching in a rural school, and about working with others.

I'll always remember the end-of-year parties, how proud the kids are of dressing up and performing the traditional songs and dances, and their excitement when we show up every week and every year. I appreciate the warm welcome and unending help from Alejandra, then the kindergarten teacher; the leadership of Lucha; and the support of all the teachers in making the program a success.

I love how much the students like coming to English class and enjoy how quickly they accept us into their lives. The parents I met are proud of their kids and always happy to talk about them. They seem to appreciate it when I introduce myself and show interest in their families. I am continually struck by how family-centered Mexico is, and how the village is a culture unto itself where everybody knows everybody else (and is probably related to them), where the kids never lack for friends, where many adults pitch in to cook meals, fix the road or do whatever needs doing. I also know that there are troubled families in Los Ricos, as well as disagreements among people in the village. Dianne does a great job of sharing information when needed, but not interfering in the community's business.

As for what I give and receive, the program gives me a sense of purpose and belonging. I need to have children in my life to feel like a whole person, and the kids of Los Ricos are a lovable bunch.

Mary Beth Sunenblick: Mexico feels like home to me. Although I come from a much different life that I treasure in Maine, I have a strong attachment to the Mexico I have come to know and love. My time is divided equally between San Miguel and Portland.

I retired from my profession as a clinical social worker in 2017. I had a fulfilling career at a teaching hospital in Portland, working with children, adolescents, families, and adults. In addition, I had a private psychotherapy practice that evolved into full-time work once I left the hospital in 2000.

I knew about Feed the Hungry, but not the Los Ricos program specifically. A friend sent out a mass email describing her Los Ricos experience as a volunteer. Upon my first visit to the community, I was hooked.

I am drawn to rural outposts where the resources are minimal, but the spirit of the communities is strong and culturally rich. Previously I participated in a team delivering primary healthcare services to poor and remote communities in the mountains of the Dominican Republic. From this program, I learned about flexibility, hard work, and small, realistic goals. This work introduced me to the equivalent of the campo in Mexico. I had no illusions!

Nothing particularly took me by surprise, other than the kids' access to orange-colored Cheetos that were then sold outside the school gates. I could understand that the kids might be hungry after their school day, but also understood that my role was to enforce the no-food rule until our hour of school time was over. This was both funny and challenging. The boys stashed their snacks in various places, with me discovering the hidden spots, and finding my own place to store the Cheetos until class time was over. The boys kept finding the hidden snacks! Eventually, I outfoxed them and held the line.

I hope to stay with the program for as long as I am needed. I like the continuity of getting to know the children, teachers, and parents. In a nutshell, it seems that the guiding principles of the program include small, realistic goals, flexibility, and the ability to roll with the punches. This suits me to a tee!

Bill Wilkinson: I became involved in rural education when I helped vet a San Miguel applicant to a scholarship program called Jóvenes Adelante eight years ago. This young woman came from abject poverty in a rural community known as El Lindero. That experience taught me how difficult it is for bright young people from impoverished rural circumstances to get the help they need for university studies.

That brief encounter was followed by driving volunteers to Los Ricos for two years. Once at the school, I was assigned to check out library books and assist in teaching junior high school students who came to after-school classes. I observed the role Lucha played in advocating for her school and enlisting help from the foreign community.

Meanwhile, I became acquainted with Emma Guera, the teacher at El Lindero, who encouraged me to organize enrichment programs there and in other rural schools. I am an organizer, not a teacher. I organized volunteer teaching programs in several schools, installed libraries with donated books organized by professional librarians, procured computers and on-site internet services for the students, as well as sundry other projects (such as nontoxic drinking water and vegetable gardens).

I have never forgotten my roots at Los Ricos and routinely keep up with all the friends that I made there. Our school programs face similar issues, and we all gain by sharing experiences, strategies, and information.

Lois Weiss: I've been thinking about why I enjoyed Los Ricos. I've never been a teacher—I'm a lawyer—but I love little kids. I had few illusions about what I could offer them academically. I just loved being with them; seeing those children laugh; showing them that white-haired gringos could be fun; trusting that at least they would remember the parts of the body—in ENGLISH.

CHAPTER 14

Los Ricos Teachers Remember Their Students

No male student from Los Ricos had ever graduated from high school when we started volunteering. Economic demands, few role models, and the expense added up to little desire to continue studying. Male teenagers soon leave school and take jobs in the fields or in construction. We witnessed many promising students try to finish but drop out along the way. One who took the lead to stay in school was José Manuel.

JOSÉ MANUEL
~ Bob Bowers

If I had all the things that Los Ricos gave me in physical form and gathered them together, they'd fill at least a small museum. As it is, there are framed photos, cards, some marbles given to me by small boys, and a drawing of a dinosaur done by a first grader that take places of honor in my house.

The two biggest gifts, though, come packaged in one boy named José Manuel. I met him in my first season at Los Ricos de Abajo. He was fifteen at the time and had dropped out of high school because he was being teased so badly about his teeth, which were twisted in his mouth and in bad shape. He took time off work every Wednesday not only to join the adult class led by Jean Degnon where I was a weekly volunteer, but also to stay and participate in the second session of classes for the high school students. He somehow always ended up in the group I happened to be working with. One week he was absent from the adult class, which was a first. We had begun without him when he joined us about fifteen minutes into the class. His lower face was covered with a bandana, which was unusual in those pre-Covid days. I learned that he had just left the traveling Patronato Pro Niños dental van and came to our class after having had some intensive dental work done. His mouth was bruised and sore, but he didn't want to miss class so he came as soon as he could. After class, I urged him to go home before all the anesthesia wore off and go to bed, but he refused. He stayed, waited an hour for the second class to begin, and participated in that one as well. By then it was clear he was suffering, but he refused to give up. I felt honored indeed that he thought whatever I had to offer was worth that price tag!

José Manuel returned to school the following fall and joined the Saturday English classes at Casa Lord as soon as they started. By the time he graduated, he had become fluent in English. His graduating class voted to have each student select a padrino, a person who had guided and motivated them to succeed in school. José Manuel asked me to participate with him. It involved going up with him when he received his diploma and being publicly honored by the community at the ceremony. I can think of few things in my life that made me feel more honored. For the record, in 2014 José Manuel was the first male to graduate high school in the entire history of Los Ricos de Abajo. The framed photo I have of that ceremony sits in a place of honor on my shelf where it makes me smile on a daily basis. As gifts go, it was and is a rare and precious thing.

ESTRELLA GETS HER PAPERS
~ Rick Hernández

Estrella, our Los Ricos shining star, is emblematic of the English program at Las Naciones Unidas Primaria School. The story is bittersweet and somehow ends happily. I firmly believe Estrella to be an exceptional person. Her intelligence, love of education, kindness, perseverance, and many other qualities are worth telling.

I first heard of Estrella, her life, her excellent elementary school performance, and her paperless status from Dianne on my first day as a volunteer teacher years ago. By paperless, I mean that since her mother didn't record her birth, she had no birth certificate and therefore no record of school attendance documents. To Lucha's credit, she had allowed Estrella to enroll without the required documentation, but that would catch up with Estrella. To complicate everything, Estrella was required by her family to work in their brick factory; hence, no time for school. When she was five, authorities removed her from the factory, but once out of elementary school, back she went.

Another reason Estrella could not proceed to secundaria was because some of her paperwork was missing, and what was there was incorrect. Since I speak Spanish and spend a good amount of time in San Miguel, I could handle the task of getting this stuff all figured out. The task would involve many visits to offices in town, to the capital city of Guanajuato and even Mexico City. I agreed. No sweat, I thought.

That same day I met Estrella. I found her to be a natural-born WOW person, a woman of wonder. We talked a bit about everything we were going to do. The mentor tutoring stuff would begin the following Sunday. I told her to get her grandmother's OK. I gave her a few pesos for the bus fare, and we agreed to meet every Sunday at a restaurant by the Jardín. Our start time was always at 11:00 a.m.

So we started. My partner, Arnold Lawrence, and I arrived at the restaurant. There she was sitting at a back table with two cousins, Karin and José Juan, who were her chaperones. All three appeared eager and happy.

We ordered breakfast, ate, and talked. Plenty of food, juice and so we bonded. Estrella proved herself to be smart and, although shy, spoke English well. Easy homework was given for the following week, and we left with the agreement that we'd meet next week. We did this Sunday tutoring mentoring whenever we were in San Miguel.

The following day, Monday, I would start the paper search. I went to see my notario thinking he'd get the paperwork resolved. I was told "we don't do that." He suggested I go to the DIF (Desarrollo Integral de la Familia), a family assistance program. There I was told to get help at an office in the city of Guanajuato. I went and got no help there. It was suggested I go to Mexico City and talk to someone at the Registro Civil. I went twice to Mexico City and got nothing.

At that point, my time was running out in San Miguel as we were getting ready to return to Detroit, Michigan. We would not be back until the fall.

Since I had made no progress on Estrella's paperwork, I went to see my attorney and his wife. They thought they could get it resolved. I hired them to just get it done. Get those damned papers.

The following Sunday I told Estrella to go to his office and give him information and her OK to start. Give him all your family names.

She went. They encountered many bureaucratic walls, but like all good Mexicans, they have connections. I would call or email the lawyer for a status every so often and then BINGO. In April of the following year, the ball started rolling and by midsummer, everything was done. Estrella was given her fresh birth record, a certificate of primary school completion, and her all-important CURP (Clave Única de Registro de Población), a card with an identification code. She was in the system.

At about this time, some GOOD people among our volunteers started to get involved for the sake of getting her into a secundaria school and finding a dentist for her.

As it turned out, the secundaria had to be a special program because Estrella was a few years older and no longer qualified for regular day school. For placement purposes, she had to take some academic competency tests. We all, including Estrella, got a surprise: she passed all her comp tests and was given a certificate stating she was eligible for prepa or, in other words, high school. Amazing. She completed secundaria in only one morning.

WOW. We had a star named Estrella.

All the while that the paperwork was being chased down, Arnold and I continued our tutoring and mentoring duties. We continued to meet at the restaurant. Breakfast was bountiful and homework completed. The restaurant manager got involved and oversaw homework, brought fresh juice non-stop, and chatted them up in English. He, like us, was proud of Estrella.

Estrella never missed a Sunday. Her escorts would change but Estrella was always there.

During this time, she met my four sisters from Detroit, many nieces/nephews, countless friends from New York City, Florida, and Phoenix. They/we loved the Sunday breakfast with the star. Estrella truly enjoyed meeting my family and friends. My sisters became her tías.

Toward the end of our Sundays, and if we had the time, we'd go wandering around town. Estrella was so fascinated and proud that San Miguel was hers.

On one special Sunday, we wandered into the Bellas Artes building. She and her chaperones had never been there. A nice docent gave them a tour of the place. Also, they met an artist who was doing a participatory exhibit involving women. She started talking to Estrella and asked her to write something about a favorite female or a future goal. She chose to write two things. One was to be a teacher someday. The artist videotaped Estrella and pinned one of her notes to the art piece.

Estrella was no longer shy. She just did this and then said her hasta luegos to the artist. At that moment and in busy Bellas Artes I saw a poised and grownup young woman … WOW.

We had a few more Sundays. Another volunteer got her a phone and we arranged to step up the tutoring. A language arts teacher jumped in to get her ready for the big time. That being prepa and then college.

Arnold and I sort of faded into the background. I'd call her occasionally. I was even introduced to her first boyfriend. We liked him. Then she happily moved on. And I learned so much about myself and what I got from Estrella, the Mexican people, and the Feed the Hungry Los Ricos volunteers.

THREE WHO WILL ALWAYS BE WITH ME
~ Doug Lord

Through all these activities I was fortunate to get to know many fine students, all of whom made lasting impressions. These are three that I have known for the longest period and who will always be with me.

Maritza: One day when we were out at the Los Ricos school, Dianne told me that there was a student who was a bit older and who had dropped out of a secondary school to help support her family. Now, she wanted to return to school and take our English classes. So, I was introduced to Maritza, whose family lived in a compound in Los Ricos near the school.

When Maritza returned to classes, she came from a job where she had been cutting up chicken parts in San Miguel. When she came to our program, she was highly motivated, more mature than some of the younger kids and really buckled down to her tasks. She was an inspiration for me; there's nothing like a motivated student.

She started taking the Saturday classes at our house and I taught her along with two or three other girls. Maritza's best friend at that time was Yessenia, who was still in high school and had already decided that she was going to become a lawyer. The two girls were also attending the computer class. They received double scholarships to run the Learning Center at the school. They also took a computer class in San Miguel, so I would see them together when they came to get tuition money for that class. They always brightened up Saturday for me because they came in full of energy, laughing and smiling. Yessenia was unable to participate in the weekly Saturday English classes because she had to work every Saturday selling religious objects for an aunt who had a small store in the sanctuary town of Atotonilco. Maritza, like many of the girls, was interested in soccer (fútbol) so she invited us to her games.

After Maritza graduated from high school, she was interested in attending university. Dianne, Maritza, and I drove to Dolores Hidalgo to visit a university. The school was known for studies in technology, which was Maritza's interest. Later, when she was planning to take the entrance exam, I planned to pick her up early in the morning, parking my car on one side of the then flooded Río Laja. She crossed the rickety foot bridge over the river, approached my car, and reported, somewhat sheepishly, that she was not going to be able to continue with that university. Perhaps it was just too much for her, too far away from home and family. Undaunted, she then decided to attend a university in San Miguel proper, closer to home (and boyfriend). She moved into the apartment in San Miguel that we had rented for the female university students and started taking technical classes. She quickly discovered that she was overwhelmed in that path and switched over to arts and graphics classes, in which she excelled in getting top grades. Maritza proudly showed me various projects that she had created. Her talent and work ethic were obvious.

Then, one day, out of the blue, she showed up at my house with her boyfriend, a nice guy named Miguel Ángel with whom she had been involved for many years. She was pregnant. They planned to move into his parents' house, as was the custom in the campo, and have a baby. I vividly remember that she asked me if I was disappointed. I mumbled something, and I hope I said that I was proud of her. We hopped in my car and drove out to where the English teachers were preparing to drive to Los Ricos, and she said her goodbyes.

Over the years since then, Maritza has returned, usually unexpectedly, to my house with her family, including her lovely little daughter Leila. She seems quite happy, having decided to have only one child because she had a particularly difficult pregnancy.

It's a big step for girls of this generation who now have access to contraception and can consciously use family planning. They have gone from a generation of families that had seven, eight, or nine children to one or two, as in her case. I recently got an email from Maritza that she and her family were fine and that she was becoming involved in early childhood education. I'm hopeful that she will find work in a professional capacity because she's bright, conscientious, dedicated, and a truly nice human being.

Yessenia: I first met Yessenia when she was in the sixth grade at Los Ricos. One of my favorite photographs is one of her taken by photographer and volunteer Billie Mercer. She's sitting in the class with a beautiful smile, ribbons in her hair, attentively listening to the teacher. When she got to high school, I remember her being in a Los Ricos English class with Geoff Hargreaves. He asked me one day if I would come and talk to the class about being a lawyer. I went and, in my halting Spanish and some English, explained what it was like and mentioned that the only indigenous president of Mexico, Benito Juárez, was a lawyer from the state of Oaxaca. Yessenia quickly mentioned that she knew that and that she wanted to be like him. We knew then that we had a serious student on our hands. Despite the difficulties of having serious family problems, she continued working on the weekends while going to junior and high school and then started full-time in law at the Universidad de Allende San Miguel. She began having difficulty with going to day classes and working, so she switched to night school and got a job with a lawyer friend of Dianne's and ours. She started working full-time for him and quickly started doing actual lawyer work even though she wasn't yet a lawyer. She's now been working for him for many years, finished the university and is waiting to get her license (cédula) to practice law.

A Facebook page seems essential for all the students we know, and Yessenia is still active on hers, posting messages saying how much she appreciates and enjoys being an attorney. She now has a baby girl, Xenia, and occasionally both come to the house for a visit. She can have the baby with her in the office, close to where she lives during the week in the SMA apartment. On the weekends, she visits her husband in the campo, where he works as a horse trainer.

In summary, Yessenia is a perfect example of what a young person can do with a goal, drive, and extremely hard work, despite serious odds.

Aidé: One of our students who did have strong family support, including a strong mother, was Aidé. When I first met her, she was in junior high school. We were visiting the school one afternoon where Aidé was in the schoolyard, kind of slouching on a bench, staring at us with what I thought was a frown—an interesting and intelligent looking one, but nevertheless a frown. I later learned the cause. She had a serious dental problem and rarely smiled. Then, an anonymous teacher contributed money toward orthodontia. Aidé would come on Saturday for English classes at my house, then go to the orthodontist to get her braces tightened. It took some years, but eventually she emerged with one of the nicest smiles in Los Ricos, a real success story for both her and for that generous teacher.

For many years, Aidé was one of our best English students in the Saturday class and she told me at one point that even though she had classes in English in junior high school, high school, and university that she really gained her fluency in those classes with Bob Bowers. When Aidé successfully finished high school and applied to Universidad de León in San Miguel, she initially agreed to live in the apartment that we had rented for the female students. After a short period of time, however, her mother discovered that there were a few beer cans (not Aidé's) in the apartment and, being a strict mother, she pulled Aidé out of the apartment; thereafter, she commuted to classes all the way into San Miguel from their new home in the city of Querétaro. She successfully graduated three years later with a degree in business administration and went to work in one of the more elegant hotels in San Miguel. Even though it was a long distance to come in on Saturdays as well as all the other days, she attended practically every Saturday class. Aidé seldom missed Saturday class for the entire time she was in university. She generously helped other students and made people laugh.

From time to time, Aidé visited me at the house with a young man in tow, who she also always introduced as a friend and not as a boyfriend, denying any romantic relationship. Recently her Facebook postings indicate that she's found the right one at last and she seems happy. Most of the Los Ricos students are transparent about their personal life online. We keep up with our students thanks to Facebook, which they call "Face."

These are just three of the many students, the ones I have known the longest, with whom I've had a wonderful relationship during my time at Los Ricos. I'm grateful to them, to Dianne and the other teachers for the opportunity to share the riches of Mexican culture and to become friends with some of the residents of Los Ricos de Abajo.

CHALLENGES
~ Dianne Walta Hart

Expectations had to be modified. We were making a difference and we knew it. Students were going on to secundaria and eventually preparatoria, but a one-hour English lesson every Wednesday for ten weeks was not going to result in a flood of proficient English speakers. What we really were doing was introducing the outside world to what had been an insular and isolated community.

The community was changing as well. The Learning Center had Wi-Fi and computers, and everyone was learning to use them. Over time, parents and eventually many students had cell phones. Students were using tablets to do their homework at the Learning Center. Driving out to the village, we often got a wave from a villager driving a truck.

Still, logistical transportation problems loomed. We were always on the lookout for volunteers with SUVs who were willing to transport teachers to Los Ricos. Not everyone wanted to face the river, the road, the potential of a standoff with the Coke truck, and the wear and tear. Nor did all the drivers want us to stash some teachers or students in the back of their vehicles for the trip back to San Miguel.

Some years we had enough volunteers and at one point we had to tell those who were volunteering for only a few weeks that we couldn't accommodate them in the classrooms, or in the cars.

Some teachers failed to develop lesson plans, leaving their classroom helpers muddled. Some didn't even try to follow our sketchy curriculum. One year we tried to project lessons developed on our laptops onto a screen, only to find out that the instability of power in Los Ricos left the teachers scrambling when nothing worked. Gradually the lessons became more imaginative, incorporating English into adventures not imagined in our early years.

As individuals and as a group, we had all those struggles and more. What united us was the importance of education. We all knew the opportunities it had provided us and the life it allowed us to live. We firmly believed that it would help our students, too, and we tried to show them the possibilities. In the early years, we weren't even considering universities or post-high school training, but thought that, especially for some students, including Estrella, every day of class was a bonus. Some took advantage of our growing expectations. Some didn't. One year we had a grade level of super achievers, and the next year most of them were gone by the eleventh grade. Again, we saw this as an achievement because eleventh grade was five more years of schooling beyond primary school. Some students we expected would shine in school, would drop out, work in the fields or in someone's home, or become young parents themselves. We even started teaching the children of our students.

After reading Jeffrey Sachs's[26] theories on the fight against poverty—one was that instead of thinly spreading the assistance to many places, agencies focus on a few areas and provide as much help as they can—we concluded that many attempts to diminish poverty were already underway in Los Ricos: Feed the Hungry was feeding the children, working on a program to nourish babies through preschool, teaching parents about nutrition, and studying the children's health. Other San Miguel NGOs in the area, such as Caminos de Agua, were working on the water, a problem all over Mexico but especially in the countryside, and we were allowing the students to become more educated. Mujeres en Cambio also assisted with young women's education, and Jovenes Adelante gave university scholarships to the most promising.

To help with medical problems, Feed the Hungry worked with Patronato Pro Niños to provide medical and dental care, and the English teachers occasionally financed dental care to older students who had lacked it throughout their childhood. The Club de Leones (Lions Club) diagnosed vision problems.

With the help of Feed the Hungry and donors, we built bathrooms, a dining room, a storage area, set up a Learning Center with computers at the school, provided a library, taught English from kindergarten through adults, provided scholarships to every student who graduated from the sixth grade through their university education, rented an apartment we dubbed The University House for students who had early morning university classes

---

[26] Jeffrey David Sachs is an American economist, academic, public policy analyst, and former director of The Earth Institute at Columbia University. He is known as one of the world's leading experts on sustainable development, economic development, and the fight against poverty. Wikipedia

on the far side of San Miguel from Los Ricos, mentored students, provided Saturday English classes at Doug Lord's house almost every Saturday of the year, sometimes found employment for them, and other times were there for them in their moments of crisis.

Occasionally, we'd run headfirst into problems that were beyond our scope, such as when we were alerted to elementary students discriminating against others for having darker skins. In that case, the teacher, Rick Hernández, brought the girl closer to him when they read outside on the patio to show his approval of her. For those few weeks, it seemed to work. Or, as one of our students later told us, students teased her for having a body image that didn't conform to the ideal. We followed Lucha's policy of not letting long-held community disputes play out in the classroom. But clearly, racism and bullying exist everywhere, even in Los Ricos.

Older students confided in us, related their missteps, but there were also times when our disappointments were voiced directly to them. Sometimes they cried, sometimes we did. Some students thrived. Some teachers did, too, but not everyone.

In many ways, the program continued because we took baby steps, grew where we saw the need, pulled back when it didn't work, and continued to show up year after year. When people ask how it worked, we tell them that. It's that simple. And that difficult.

THE NACIONES UNIDAS FIESTA: A TIME FOR EVERYTHING UNDER THE SUN
~ Carolyn Simsarian

Mexican culture, in secular life as well as religious life, marks and honors the beginning and the end. Our last day of teaching is always the week before Easter, and the fiesta at last session is the celebration of all that has been accomplished—books read, vocabulary learned, motivational speeches given, advice and encouragement offered and hopefully received.

The fiesta is the ultimate reciprocal gift. Everyone in the village participates and contributes to this special event. The scholarship students from the junior and senior high schools in Atotonilco have rushed back to secure their spot sitting on the bank under the mesquite tree. Moms with bundled babies, aunts with preschoolers in tow, and grandmothers, in clean aprons, hair gathered in one braid, are seated in folding chairs. Grandfathers, dads, and uncles who are able are in attendance. Long tables have been set up under the covered patio where posters of student projects decorate the windows of the classrooms. There are colorful balloons and festoons of crepe paper. The red, green, and white Mexican flag with eagle and serpent flaps proudly against the flagpole.

Lucha has everything orchestrated and choreographed beginning with a well-organized program. First, the teachers honor each grade for their participation in the tutoring project. In the past, sixth grade usually marked the end of one's formal education.

On this day we celebrate with the village. The sixth graders, resplendent in their school uniforms of navy skirts or pants, navy sweater, white blouse or shirt, receive a certificate and an English-Spanish dictionary in recognition of their achievement. It is a proud moment.

No fiesta in Mexico is complete without music and dancing. Mexican folk dances, recognized around the world, are emblematic of their states of origin. After the speeches and presentations, the various grades assemble on the sides of the basketball court, ready to show their skills at what took weeks to perfect.

Each grade group has mastered the steps of the dance and is dressed in the appropriate costume. We are treated to La Danza de Los Viejitos (the Dance of the Little Old Men) from the state of Michoacán. Masked with the faces of old men, the third- and fourth-grade dancers wear traditional straw hats with multicolored ribbons streaming from the crown, extending over the rims. Ponchos and white cotton trousers complete the costume. The "old men" lean heavily on their canes and hold their aching backs as they struggle around the stage. The music intensifies; they pick up the pace. Soon the canes are thrown down and they dance with the vigor of youth! It cannot last. The music slows, they pick up their canes, and slowly hobble off stage. We must accept what comes with living a long life.

Jalisco, the state where mariachi music originated, is another source of many traditional Mexican folk dances. The fifth- and sixth-grade girls appear on stage dressed in colorful, ribboned skirts and blouses, their hair styled into lustrous braids adorned with ribbons. The sweeping skirts in bright orange, green, and pink are extended to each side at arm's length, butterflies about to take flight. Dressed in black pants and white shirts, the boys emerge to join their partners. They wear red kerchiefs on their heads, tied back like a pirate. Each hand holds a short wooden sword. They whirl, strike the ground with the sword, whirl in the opposite direction, again striking the ground. The clacking sound of striking swords synchronizes with exuberant music reenacting a sword fight. The dancers take their well-earned bows to the applause of an appreciative audience. Everyone is beaming.

Just as vital as music and dancing, the food or comida is the grand finale of the celebration. The women of the village bring kettles of rice, handmade tortillas, and the star of the meal, chicken with mole sauce. Mole, a dark complex sauce, contains multiple ingredients including ground seeds and spices, as well as a touch of chocolate, and is a special occasion tradition served at weddings and baptisms. Rich and flavorful, we all feel honored to enjoy this superb dish—the best we've ever tasted.

The volunteers contribute a treat to this grand finale—three large chocolate cakes, decorated with frosting flags of Mexico, Canada, and the United States, symbolizing the many participants in the program and the name of the school—Escuela Primaria Naciones Unidos. Young and old alike line up to be served a slice of pastel. Sometimes more than once.

FEEDING AND TEACHING
~ Dianne Walta Hart

Our older students look back to the days before the pandemic and talk about their traditional food and the food from Feed the Hungry's kitchen in Los Ricos.

Yessenia says that "at home, our food was almost always beans, rice, lentils, soups, and on rare occasions, we ate meat, but we had a lot of fruit because we had fruit trees. I remember when Feed the Hungry came to the community that the food was good and nutritious. They helped us understand that it was important to eat healthily. Since then, my brother Luis Antonio asks every person who is eating if it is healthy or nutritious. The food helped my mother because she no longer had to worry about our lunch because she knew that we ate well at school."

Alejandro talks about the traditional food from his Los Ricos childhood that he loved, starting with mole, the Los Ricos version adored by all the teachers. "I really don't have a favorite food but if I had to choose, it would be mole. If I were to cook, I would make typical dishes from my community: mole, chicken, pork, fish, gorditas (they include several guisados), pozole, chicken soup, pumpkins, potatoes. There are many combinations that can be made with what little there is in my community."

But Claudia mentions the adjustment to new food, when she mentioned that "some foods made by the Feed the Hungry cooks I didn't like, and the teachers told me they were important for my health. I didn't understand it then but now I know it was for my own good, each food has different proteins that help our body to be healthy."

One of the reasons for Feed the Hungry's presence is to help students learn, precisely the point made by Rosa Elena. "I don't remember the exact date or year in which the Feed the Hungry program came to Los Ricos, I only remember that the food was exquisite: chickpeas, rice, vegetable soup, lentils, everything that satisfies the stomach. We paid more attention in the classes, and it helped us learn about nutrition."

Years before the pandemic, Chef Gerardo Ramos[27] talked with the fifth and sixth graders, and volunteer Joan Mitchell wrote about it for a local newspaper.[28] She described how the teachers had been focusing on the words for dozens of vegetables, herbs, garden tools, gardening tasks, all leading up to his demonstration. He showed them a "a graph that tells them how much sugar they consume every time they drink a refresco or a fruit juice, and how too much sugar is not good for them, because it gives them spikes of energy that are followed by steep declines that can prevent them from concentrating, focusing, learning."

After a comida of "cannelloni filled with a delicious mixture of chopped fresh vegetables, garnished with more fresh vegetables, and served with a marinara sauce," he discussed nutrition, and much to everyone's surprise, followed that up by making dessert: a beet lollipop.

Gerardo continued, but with a life lesson. He "told the children about himself, too; how he grew up in Michoacán, in a pueblito not unlike theirs, and went to a school maybe like theirs; how he always knew he wanted to make the best possible life for himself; how he had the opportunity to learn to cook, to become a chef, to work in restaurants in Atlanta for 11 years before returning to Mexico. When he went to the United States, he knew not a word of English and that they should take advantage of every minute they have with their volunteer English teachers, because they never know when they might have an opportunity that would only arise because they know some English."

Knowing another language worked its way into the Feed the Hungry organization. At a Feed the Hungry party for volunteers, Giff Moody from the board mentioned what he described as his win-win idea. Feed the Hungry, with its primarily English-speaking board, needed to communicate with its

---

[27] Gerardo Ramos was a chef at San Miguel's Café Firenze at the time of the article; now he's in Mexico City at Havre 77.

[28] "Food, Food, and More Food: Beet Lollipops at Los Ricos de Abajo" by Joan Mitchell, Atención San Miguel, 2013.

staff members more easily. The board had varying degrees of Spanish proficiency, but what if they also provided English for their employees. And what if, instead of hiring teachers outside of Feed the Hungry, they asked some of the Los Ricos volunteers to teach English and then their payments would go to the Los Ricos scholarship fund? Great idea was my response, and to the rescue came Rick Hernández, Bob Bowers, Ezequiel Ruiz, Suzanne Bacon, and Lyne Daroff.

Suzanne, who says she had "neither the skills nor the materials to teach in the traditional second-language way," decided to emphasize vocabulary. "I collected sources with cooking terminology, good shopping terms, and expressions to describe food and restaurant vocabulary. We had fun with all this material for a few classes, and I was learning with them. Then I had an idea that we should cook together in English. We had the perfect kitchen at Feed the Hungry and a group of people who enjoyed food and each other. I lamely chose a simple and unsophisticated recipe for miniature Reuben sandwiches. I brought some of the ingredients from the United States because I thought I would not be able to find them here, like mini-rye bread. Wrong on both counts. The recipe was complicated because of the English expressions which did not translate easily into Spanish, and it was poorly written to boot! That's what made the class so successful. We debated what a particular sentence meant. We made the sandwiches, and all sat down at a long table to enjoy them.

"The second recipe we chose together was from a bilingual cookbook called *North of the Border*. It was zucchini ratatouille, but we added sausage and Mexican flavoring to make it more interesting. Again, a huge success. Every student was engaged, had fun, and we got to eat together at the end. We also invited others who were in the office.

"We were then interrupted by the break for Semana Santa. Covid hit about the same time and our classroom shut down. Instead of planning and provisioning weekly lunches for the elementary schools, the staff had to reengineer their jobs to provide entire communities with the raw materials to feed whole families, not just the school children. They had to work without the volunteers who are largely an older expat community and among the most vulnerable to Covid. They had to follow strict Covid protocols to ensure the communities they served were safe along with themselves. The entire organization from accounting to transportation was turned upside down."

Part 6

ACCOMPLISHMENTS AND CONTINUITY

CHAPTER 15

Where We Are Now

Mexican and foreigners alike advised us when we started offering university scholarships that rural students would study in San Miguel but that they'd never study nor work far from home. The countryside was what the students were familiar with and that's where they'd return. By and large, that's true, but early on, **Yessenia** hoped to go to law school at the Universidad de Guanajuato, an hour away. She didn't get in, and we were already recognizing that she was more adventurous than most, so we assumed the stay-close-to-home adage would continue.

But then **Rosa Elena** did an internship in Cancún, followed by another one in Heredia, Costa Rica. Today brothers **Alexis** and **Eric Yahir** are both interested in science and attending universities in nearby Celaya. **Luis Ángel** is a veterinary student at Universidad del La Salle Bajío in León and **José Miguel** studies accounting at Universidad Patria in Dolores Hidalgo, all in the state of Guanajuato. **Yessenia** continues her studies in Querétaro. University students, both male and female, often rented rooms near their universities, be they in Celaya, Dolores Hidalgo, León, or San Miguel, but again, while they're adventurous enough to leave San Miguel, staying close to home was a goal of all of them.

When they begin their professional lives, they often return to San Miguel de Allende and find homes either there, in Los Ricos, or the nearby rural communities. Tradition has had it that women go to where their husbands grew up and often, but not always, that's the case, and might change even more in the future.

According to statistics, in 2005 Los Ricos had 220 people, but in 2020, 480. That's not due to lots of babies being born, however, since the fertility rate per woman in 2010 was 13.95 and in 2020 it was 2.46. We see that playing out in our students' lives. We are happy to note that in 2010, the average years of schooling was 5.03 and ten years later it was 7.16.[29]

As for our university graduates, most of our first group were ready to enter the workforce around the time the pandemic began. It slowed them down, and many lowered their expectations. Other students decided to challenge it head on. **Cynthia**, for example, who had finished massage therapy school, finished a certificate in elder care. **Rosa Elena** lives in Tierra Blanca de Arriba, a rural community, with Rafael, the father of her daughter, Ilse Guadalupe, but just before the pandemic, she started a small travel agency and hopes to begin again.

Our first high school graduates, **Alejandro** and **José Miguel** stayed close to home. Alejandro is married to Gabriela, they have two children, and live in El Salto, a small community not far from Los Ricos where he works in a plant. José Manuel makes his home in Los Ricos with his girlfriend, and he works in construction.

Aidé works as an administrator in a San Miguel flooring store and has a second job managing the family construction business—her mother's husband is an architect. Aidé lives in San Miguel de Allende with them. **María Maritza** lives outside San Miguel in Las Cañas with her husband and daughter and is a promoter of Beginning Education (Educación Inicial).[30] This allows her to work from home, to feel useful, and at the same time, be able to spend time with her daughter. **Maria José** has her university degree and works in San Miguel. So does **Leticia**, who graduated from Instituto Tecnológico Sanmiguelense de Estudios Superiores in Business Management and works for the county administration. She continues to spend time with her girlfriend, Cristina.

Laura Jimena hopes to be a "great agronomist" because that's what she's studying at Universidad Tecnológica de San Miguel de Allende. **Alfredo** studies nutrition at the Universidad Tecnológica de San Miguel de Allende. **Claudia**, a high school graduate, works for a San Miguel export company. **Mariana** studies nursing in San Miguel and Lupe is at the Universidad de León in San Miguel.

Agustín is a United States citizen and serves with the United States Army. As of this writing, he had been in Poland and South Korea, and is presently receiving more training in Fort Lee, Virginia. His brother **Fernando** was the first Los Ricos male student to graduate from a university.

---

[29] https://en.mexico.pueblosamerica.com/i/los-ricos-de-abajo-los-ricos/

[30] Educación Inicial is a state-wide program to work with students under the age of four.

Estrella (by Jean Degnon): One of the most poignant and sweet stories is that of Estrella. I first met her when I taught third grade. She was smart and feisty. We found out that she had been working at a brick factory as a six-year-old and living with her abuelita, owner of the brick factory. Somewhere along the line, she disappeared, and I lost touch with her. Years later, she reappeared, like a beautiful butterfly, a lovely, confident teenager. We celebrated her sixteenth birthday with carrot cake in the adult class, which she attended for several years. Because of some bureaucratic hang-ups (no birth certificate), she was prevented from attending regular school. Rick Hernández was crucial in obtaining credentials for her. After a couple of years, she disappeared again. Recently, however, I ran into her at the bus stop with her adorable baby son, whom she proudly showed off. She seems happy and is in touch with several of us on Facebook, and she phones Rick on occasion.

Bob Haas, who picked up Lucha in the truck, died 2013.

Michael Chadwick continues to support the school and the scholarship program.

AND...
LUCHA AND YESSENIA

Lucha: When you come from a large, humble, and extremely poor family like mine, you know you are not allowed to abandon yourself to suffering, nor do you have time to grieve or lick your wounds. As I grew up, I saw that teachers ate food that I had never seen before, and that's what motivated me to study, get ahead, become a teacher, and help others. Then, after I lost that battle against death, I felt that I would also die, but coming from my family also taught me to survive in the middle of those dozen children my mother had. And I learned that when suddenly the world seems to spin backwards, you must again fight for what you want to achieve. When I returned from Mexico City after Guillermo died, I had to face the reality that my son was no longer here and there were many things to resolve.

My heart started to die when my dear son's heart stopped beating, but I didn't sit down to cry because he needs me alive. Even though I feel my heart dying little by little, the rest of my being struggles to live. This heart of mine was divided into three equal parts, one of them has died—it stopped existing—but before leaving it left a small piece behind that is growing and asking for my help in everything. I have to get on my feet when life seems too difficult, especially during the pandemic that has changed the economy, health, hygiene, food, and education for everyone, but I have to remember that I have the other two parts of my heart—José Eduardo and Luis Fernando—and even though they're grown up, they're a reason to keep praying, to keep believing, to keep trusting, to keep fighting … and to keep living.

There are moments of nostalgia and sadness when I'd like not to be me, when I'd like to avoid reality. But then I turn around and see my grandson Guillermo Sebastián and I raise my eyes to the heavens and ask God for more time, more time to enjoy his beautiful smile and the joy that he exudes, time to see him run around the house and play, to help him with what he needs, to watch him grow up. I also ask for time to see the direction that Eduardo and Fernando pursue.

My life has been spent in a country where its people are warm and affectionate, which is why my writing may seem overly sentimental, but I am a loving mother and close to my children. For me love is essential in a family, at work, and in society. All the struggles I've had to live with and the battles I've had to face—even though I haven't won them all—have taught me to continue standing and living and showing my grandson, my children, my family, and the world my joy and happiness to be with them and with having each other. I am grateful to be alive and in good health after having faced that virus without any vaccine. The sadness, yes, I carry that inside and only God and I know how deep it is in my being. I've lived through unforgettable things with all of you, and I thank you for supporting me in this stage of my life.

Yessenia: For a long time, I have felt that I was stuck at work. I've always wanted to be a trial attorney, so I quit my job. The next step is that I am going to be a partner of Estefania (Fanny) who is my friend from the university and who has finished two master's degrees. Our step together is to litigate on our own without having a boss. It will not be easy, we know, but we want to be excellent lawyers, and I know that in time we will have a better firm and many clients. I also decided to continue learning and have started a master's degree in criminal law at the Centro de Estudios Superiores del Bajío in Querétaro. I live outside San Miguel in Montecillo de Nieto with my husband and daughter.

CHAPTER 16

The Pandemic

In late March 2020, when the Secretary of Education announced the closing of public schools due to the pandemic, the school meals program and our volunteer teaching program were disrupted as well. While we continued to raise scholarship funds for students who studied online or remotely, Feed the Hungry had to find another way to aid the communities they typically support.

What they did was to retool all their activity to distribute food to the entire families of the children whom they normally serve. They turned their business model upside down. Every aspect of operations was affected: food procurement, packaging, delivering, identifying beneficiaries, and more.

Without their usual volunteer packers and drivers, staff workload increased. Vacations were cancelled. Everyone was doing their share and then some.

Irving Ayala, head of nutrition for Feed the Hungry, reported, "Everything happened suddenly. Schools closed; there were no services. We had to stop doing what was working. We normally keep a registry of the students who receive food, but not of the mothers, so we began the challenging task of assembling a list of parents which we need to organize the mothers so that they could receive food deliveries."

Coordination through the municipality's Dirección de Cultura y Tradiciones garnered support for the operation; the city provided trucks and drivers to help with the distribution of food pantries in each community. Every morning they loaded more than five tons of food on their trucks and sent out to visit a rotation of the communities. Weekly deliveries of food pantries provided critical nutrition to children and adults in need. Each twelve-kilo food pantry had enough nutritional value for a family of five to make up to ten meals each day for fourteen days. They delivered smaller sized bags of five kilos and basic cleaning supplies to the elderly and smaller families.

Volunteer Jean Degnon spoke for all the volunteers when she wrote about the pandemic. "Covid, of course, wreaked havoc with the entire program, as it has with everyone's lives. The kitchen was not operating for a while but Feed the Hungry continued to deliver food. And who knows if the people in my adult class who found jobs, like Jorge, Norma, and Andrea, have been able to sustain themselves? However, despite the pandemic, there is progress. Many families now have telephones, or students use the computers at the Learning Center. Facebook, for all its faults, connects people. I recently received birthday wishes from several of my sweet students. They post pictures of their kids' graduations and quinceañeras. As things slowly reopen, I hope to bump into them at open markets or the bus stop. May we all be able to sit and talk and laugh with one another once again!"

Every winter during the pandemic, Suzanne Bacon showed up at Los Ricos with Feed the Hungry to give the families our gift bags. She wrote, "In 2022, the final bag count was 61 combined with a donation of hats and scarves from the knitters of San Miguel. We had soccer balls, stuffed animals, tea sets, books, pencils, crayons, hot wheels, mandarinas, and a few sweets. Christie McCue and I loaded the bags into her car and drove out to Feed the Hungry where the staff loaded the food. We transferred the gift bags and hats and off we went with two trucks of food despensas, supplies and gifts. I was particularly happy to see some of the staff members with whom Lyne and I were teaching at Feed the Hungry before Covid shut us down.

"We stopped at the school where only the first- and second-grade classroom was in use. The teacher explained that the other two teachers were getting their boosters today and so the other primary students had stayed home. We were not permitted to visit the children, but they knew who we were. We left them with the two bags of hats and scarves for the primary grades.

"Up the hill beyond the kinder building, the mothers were lined up awaiting our arrival. Olivia gave a short explanation about who we were and what we brought. Two of the mothers made short thank you speeches and blessed us for all we've done for them. Some clapped and Christie and I had tears in our eyes. Valentín read off each name and the mothers came up one by one to pick up their goods. Many had babies in their arms.

"When we were finished, we drove back to kinder building and there she was, our wonderful Janet Alejandra Bautista who is the best kinder teacher ever. The children were hanging on the fencing and were so curious to see us. I did not recognize any of them. It has been so long. We explained that we had unclaimed bags and hats meant for the kinder. She unlocked the gate and accepted our gifts.

"I cannot thank you enough for your participation in round two of giving out these family gift bags. Rick and I did the shopping. I had donations of money, books, hot wheels, and pencils. Rick provided all the bags and the mandarinas. I did the assembly just because it was easier and safer that way. So many offered to help and wanted to go out to Los Ricos. I really didn't expect to see any children and the road was rougher in unexpected places. The vado is beautiful and functional. Yes, we delivered 61 gift bags and 100 hats and scarves. But what was really delivered was the reassurance that we are still here, still waiting to return and still missing these beautiful children. From the expressions on the mothers' faces and their words of thanks, I know they got the message."

CHAPTER 17

Our Return, Spring 2022

We had planned to just take as many as would fit in a CRV, but word spread, soon five volunteers became seven. It would be our first visit to Los Ricos since the pandemic curtailed the 2020 program. Suzanne and Rick had been out delivering holiday bags for each family on Three Kings Day in January. Since Dianne was in town, a reunion was anticipated for twenty-two volunteers at El Rinconcito that Wednesday evening.

The drill was to hire a van to accommodate the seven, to meet at the bakery, to pick up the chocolate sheet cakes, and to drive to Los Ricos. There would not be any formal meeting with students. We would drop off the cakes, peek in the library, and head back to town. We were going home again if only for a short visit. Suzanne stressed the actual time would be no more than thirty minutes at the school.

A bright beautiful day found us commenting on changes en route. A new housing development here, an upscale vineyard there. We turned off the paved road onto the dirt road to Los Ricos. The huisache trees along the road seemed to have grown, overarching the washboard dirt track.

Soon we reached the Río Laja. There was the vado strong and well-built with its buttressed fieldstone sides. The previous rainy season had been abundant and the vado had held its own with water pouring through its substantial conduits. Metal fittings were in place on the road surface to hold guardrails should money ever become available to finish the job. We chatted, remembering the way the families planned and contributed to its construction. First, they collected piles of rock at the river's edge, each pile representing a family's contribution. In this way, the village contributed the materials, and the city of San Miguel supplied the labor. Plenty of labor had been expended by the families gathering those piles of large heavy rocks. Seeing the vado reminded me of the year we crossed the foot bridge with teaching supplies to reach the village.

At the lower village, we made the left turn to notice which houses had improved since our last visit. Perhaps a house had been stuccoed or received a new coat of paint, or an upstairs addition had been added. The church with its Spanish bell tower looked resplendent in a fresh coat of white paint on the building and its surrounding wall.

Students were in their classrooms completing their morning lessons. They stayed on task as we peeked in from a distance. We visited the kitchen and were happy to greet the former cook Alma and other women whose children we had taught. We peeked in the Learning Center where everything was neatly in order, the shelves all dusted, the books arranged on the shelves, the nylon book bags stashed beneath. With its Wi-Fi availability, this center is truly an ongoing resource to the students of Los Ricos. Our big plastic tubs of school supplies were stacked off to the side. We hope next year that they will once again be back in use.

So that was it. We made our visit, and now it was time to leave. Not so fast. The mothers have prepared lunch for us. We were not expecting this, but how could we refuse? Into the comedor we filed. At each place, we set the traditional fiesta meal of chicken, rice, and the famous Los Ricos mole and tortillas. We sat, we ate, feeling overwhelmed with gratitude. The tradition of the final fiesta was still going forward.

As we were leaving, the children were lined up in perfect order patiently waiting to receive their slice of chocolate cake with chocolate icing. The smiles were huge. Three cakes each with an icing flag of Mexico, Canada, or the United States represented the friendship of these North American neighbors and the school appropriately named Naciones Unidas.

At last, it was time. Reluctantly, we climbed into the van. Those who had taught the kinder class felt sad to leave without saying hello. But wait, who is that waving from behind the kinder fence up on the hill. Why, it was Alejandra, the kinder teacher, in a bright yellow shirt, with arms extended waving wildly, wanting us to come and see her. Her question, "Why didn't you tell me you were coming?!" Climbing back in the bus, John commented, "Oh, this takes me back to the days when we were teaching and had such a good time in kinder!" We remembered the exuberance of the kids and the gratitude of the English teachers whose job sometimes included crawling under a table to retrieve a reluctant learner.

Bob Bowers had sent word that he was going to be in the village, and there was José Manuel who had come to say hello with his lovely wife and, on a leash, the family dog. Exchanging smiles, greetings, a few brief moments to catch up and find that all is well. Then we were off, hoping we will return, perhaps next year. If not us, perhaps we can find a fresh crop of volunteers looking for a little adventure, rewarding ways to contribute, and connection to a rural community and its people.

CHAPTER 18

As One Chapter Closes, Another Opens

As we head into the eighteenth year of the English Program at Los Ricos de Abajo, it is a joy to look back at when we started and recognize what we—and the village— did. The once almost inaccessible community now has a bridge of sorts, making trips to and from the outside world infinitely easier. Finding work has become easier, too, and it shows in homes that flash new metal doors and fresh paint. The topography and rain continue to make the roads a challenge, but volunteers have become adept at steering to the right and then quickly to the left to avoid deep trenches. From the school perched on the hill, English teachers found beauty as they look out at the homes and distant hillsides.

When we began, only half of the sixth graders continued to the seventh grade, but now all of them do. Even though not all students keep going to school after the ninth grade—economic and family concerns change many of their plans—they're better educated than they would have been had we not crossed the river and entered their lives.

No boys had ever graduated from high school, but now many of them do. No one in the community had a university degree, but now close to ten of them do, with many more right behind them.

Even though they had little access to books given their economic situations, the library opened the world of reading to them, and many grew into avid readers.

Many of our university graduates no longer live in Los Ricos, but most are in the area, and they look back at their childhood with wonder and hope for the same for their children.

Most of us, the Los Ricos volunteers, came from English-speaking countries and had a variety of career paths, many of which required advanced education. We knew that education, in its broadest sense of personal growth and development, allowed us to live our best lives and to choose rewarding career paths. The circumstances of our lives gifted us with that education and now we can give back and share this opportunity with others.

We, the volunteers, have changed, too, by achieving a greater understanding of rural Mexican culture: its richness, contradictions, beauty, and difficulties. The love goes both ways across the river.

What we didn't understand at the beginning was the power of collaboration. Yes, we thought we would enjoy getting out into rural Mexico, learning about the culture of village life, and perhaps helping kids in the process. We did not expect to be embraced by the community, to make true and long-lasting friends, and see the community grow with us in the circle of giving and receiving.

We were there as educators, facilitators, and at times, mentors. We planted seeds and ideas and gave encouragement and scholarship support, but without the cooperation of the community, the seeds would have fallen on fallow ground. The families supported us, especially as it became apparent that we were helping their children and we were there to stay, and showed it in the smiles of a mother who oversaw the opening of the school gates, of those who made us chicken, rice, and the famous Los Ricos mole for lunch, in the closing fiesta with its music and dance, and especially when they led us by the hand to dance with them.

Although we pay the bills to get the students through school, the students are the ones showing initiative to break the barriers that existed for decades by studying in middle school and high school, gathering career information, and following through with applications and entrance exams. They get up early, show up for class on time, study the material, and earn good grades, all with the support of their families and us.

Whatever has been accomplished at Los Ricos de Abajo has been a collaborative effort between the community, the school, its teachers, and the volunteer English teachers. We also had the advantage of working under the umbrella of Feed the Hungry San Miguel, which introduced us to the community, allowed us to bask in the respect granted by such a well-known NGO, and permitted our donors to deduct their gifts.

There was a slowdown during Covid, but scholarships continued and now, the in-person teaching has begun again, using the goodwill and intentions that had preceded it. New leaders stepped up and others away.

People tell us what we did could be a template for other programs, no matter what they're trying to accomplish, and others have begun. Our only advice is that we took baby steps, grew where we saw the need, pulled back when something didn't work, and continued to show up year after year.

Opportunities are still there, be they in Central Mexico or elsewhere in the world, where students and families need resources and encouragement to achieve their goals.

It is our hope that this project and book will inspire those who hope to offer those resources and encouragement to follow their hearts, and their path—no matter how daunting that road may look at first.

We promise you—the rewards are enormous.

ADDENDUM:
A NEW BEGINNING 2023

By January 2023, the world pandemic seemed to be diminishing. Students in Los Ricos had been back in school since September. With a new principal and teachers at the school, the Los Ricos English Project was welcomed back again. We needed new volunteer teachers and the all-important new drivers. Suzanne Bacon with her stellar planning ability and people skills took over leadership of the program assisted by Alice Verhoeven, mapping out the transportation. Experienced volunteers returned joined by a cadre of new eager recruits. Once again, the program was up and running.

The wrap-up meeting at the program's end is always important to assess how it all went—what were the successes and where do we need to improve. Everyone shared his/her experience of the program, the lows and the highs. Moments of joy when kinder students received their library books, moments of frustration when teachers wished their Spanish language skills were better, moments of great pride when a returning university student shared his educational journey with the class, and great sharing when mothers took our hands to come out and dance with them at the closing fiesta.

It was great to be back, to be with students once again, to plan and respond to the new challenges that inevitably arise, and to enjoy the dance with this beautiful village.

On to the nineteenth year.

Our Pre-Pandemic Schedule

Every Wednesday from mid-January until the week before Semana Santa, we follow the same schedule:

- We first teach the kindergarten students (ages three to five) in the nearby kindergarten building.
- Next, we teach the students in the elementary school (grades one through six) in the three classrooms, allow them to check out their library books, and at the same time teach the adult class in the comedor.
- We enjoy the lunch made by the Naciones Unidas mothers.
- Following that, we provide juice and cookies for the incoming junior and senior high school students.
- Then we teach those students.
- After that, we drive back to San Miguel.
- A long day.

Saturday classes take place at noon at Doug Lord's house, after which Bob Bowers sends out a Saturday's Adventure newsletter to the teachers. The Learning Center at Naciones Unidas is open three days a week and managed by three of our high school students.

MISSION STATEMENT AND OBJECTIVES FOR LOS RICOS DE ABAJO VOLUNTEER TEACHING PROGRAM: 2020

The Los Ricos Volunteer Teaching Program aims to foster a positive atmosphere for learning. Its goal is to support learning through instruction, tutoring, and scholarships. It hopes to open the doors to opportunity for the young people of Los Ricos.

The volunteers teach the students the basics of English conversation used in daily life. In **kindergarten and the first and second grades,** we focus on numbers, colors, body parts, clothing, greetings, leave-takings, songs, commands, and the use of several simple verbs. In the **third and fourth grades,** we build on the lessons of the first and second grades and add vocabulary and simple sentence structures. The **fifth and sixth grades** work on creating more complex sentences and questions using vocabulary covered in one through four plus additional words that seem appropriate. English is reinforced in the **library and the adult class.**

As the students advance in their schooling (**secundaria and Bachillerato/pre-paratoria**), the teachers continue to:

- Introduce basic English vocabulary in the following areas: greetings, colors, numbers, family, body parts, feelings, clothes, foods, home, school, city, jobs, animals, calendar, weather, and seasons.
- Review and introduce more vocabulary in the higher grades related to hobbies, sports, career interests, world geography, and current events, along with power verbs such as: have, be, like, need, want, can, do, and verbs of movement.
- Introduce older students to past and future tenses and continue to build skills through conversation, drama, guided writing, sentence creation, and creative writing.
- Encourage reading through maintenance of the library, providing Spanish, English, and bilingual books to the students.
- Develop computer literacy through the maintenance of the Learning Center (LC). Older students will be trained and hired to run the LC.
- Offer opportunities for year-round tutoring to scholarship students (equivalent to junior and senior high school).
- Encourage older students to explore post-high school education and career opportunities in San Miguel and surrounding areas.
- Provide mentoring when possible.

Responsibilities of the Lead Teachers:
- Develop lesson plans for every week.
Email the lesson plans to teaching assistants by Monday of each week.

Responsibilities of Assistants:
- Read and understand what your role is for the week.
- Contact lead teachers for clarification if necessary.
Enjoy the students and have fun. They may not remember all the English we try to teach them, but they will remember the experience.

POSTSCRIPT

PEOPLE ASK: WHERE IS LOS RICOS?
THE ANSWER: OUT BY ATOTONILCO

No story about Los Ricos can be told without mentioning the town where most students attend school starting with the seventh grade.

The first piece relates Yessenia's move to Atotonilco when she moved in with her godparents in the seventh grade and then worked in their tourist stall called a puesto. The next one talks about some Los Ricos women who are also vendors in stalls.

Yessenia's recollection of working in a puesto and a news report of Los Ricos women entrepreneurs selling food show the World Heritage site, Atotonilco, from the eyes of people in Los Ricos.

~

El Santuario de Atotonilco means Place of Hot Water/Lugar de Agua Caliente because hot water abounds in this place. When I was living there, I learned from people in Atotonilco—often called simply El Santuario—that hundreds of years ago, Father Luis Felipe Neri de Alfaro, the priest at the Oratorio church in San Miguel de Allende (at that time called San Miguel el Grande) was coming from nearby Dolores Hidalgo one day when he stopped to nap under the shade of a mesquite tree. While doing so, Jesús the Nazarene appeared in the priest's dream and asked him to build a church at that spot. Father Neri then went to the property owner, Ignacio García, bought the land, and began construction of the church on May 1, 1740. People say that the devil interfered with the construction so often that the church wasn't completed until about 1763. A painter, Miguel Antonio Martínez de Pocasangre, did the church murals, along with some verses or poems from Father Neri.

The article by Yessenia follows: Ever since, the adjoining Casa Santa de Ejercicios has housed believers of the Catholic religion, many of whom come from all over the world to attend a week-long retreat to purify their spirits, repent their sins, and find forgiveness.

When I was young, my papá used to tell me that as a young child he did a retreat in the Casa Santa de Ejercicios and saw some people who had gone crazy, people who couldn't tolerate the retreat, the confinement. He said the devil wouldn't let them finish. He also said there were some pools of water that served to purify the soul, and that before the Casa was a holy house, there were springs at the site where the Chichimecas[31] performed acts of flagellation in honor of the gods that they worshiped. Father Neri combined these Chichimeca rituals with those that San Ignacio de Loyola[32] had used to purify the body and soul. Unfortunately, those pools no longer exist in the Casa Santa de Ejercicios because there were some deaths. Or so they say. It could also be historical fiction.

When I was eight years old, I worked in Atotonilco with my former preschool teacher, Lupita, which is how I learned that the schedules of the spiritual retreats are put on a calendar that the church priest sells to the merchants so that they know when the faithful will come to Atotonilco. During those periods, Lupita sold atole and tamales and sometimes we were allowed inside the Casa Santa de Ejercicios to sell to the religious brothers or hermanos by calling: ¡Va a querer tamal, hermanito! ¡Va a querer tamales, hermanito! Lupita also sold water, items of personal hygiene such as soaps, sponges, shampoos, and a few religious things. Other times, I stayed outside where we had put blankets over a piece of wood that then we placed on two iron bases; on that, we displayed our items for sale. I still remember the euphoria of calling out as I tried to sell things: ¡pásele hermanito, tenemos agua! ¡pásele hermanito, no olvide comprar su champú, su jabón! In the afternoon when we finished, I put things in boxes, loaded them on the front of a bike, and took everything back to Lupita's house.

When I stopped working with Lupita and started working with my godparents, at first all I did was take care of the grandchildren or help with the household chores; later I set up their puesto near the church where some portals are located. My godparents had a lot of merchandise in an extremely large puesto—the largest in Atotonilco—that took half a day to put together.

First, I need to explain some of the items that we sold: sogas, disciplinas, alabanzas, and niños dioses:

---

[31] Chichimeca is the name that the Nahua peoples of Mexico generically applied to nomadic and semi-nomadic peoples who were established in present-day Bajío region of Mexico. Wikipedia.

[32] The sanctuary has been one of the principal places in Mexico to practice the spiritual exercises of Ignatius of Loyola, which include mortification of the flesh through flagellation and fasting. Wikipedia.

- The soga or rope is made of ishte, a fiber that comes from the maguey plant and is painted in colors, mainly purple, and hangs around a person's neck with a knot at the chest, which is where the Christ on a cross is inserted.
- The Christs were sold separately, the largest being around sixteen to eighteen centimeters. To get the Christ to stay on the soga, we used pliers called alicatas to make the process a little easier, but it's a challenge.
- The Christs are also used in conjunction with the disciplina for self-flagellation. The disciplina is a whip that consists of a wooden handle with seven strings that represent the seven deadly sins and the seven virtues. With this, the people at the retreat whip themselves on their backs to subdue their bodies, all according to the severity of their sins.
- The alabanzas or praises to be sung during the week are in a small blue book that has the image of the Virgin de la Luz—it doesn't have many alabanzas, but it's followed by a medium-size book with the same title and with alabanzas that are sung in the Santuario of Atotonilco.[33] The third book is even thicker with the same title and the Image of Father Neri.
- Niños dioses are babies who represent the baby Jesús and are made with plaster—I had to be especially careful because if they fell, little could be done for their restoration. On December 24th, the niños dioses are put in a manger, and the people who have them attend a Mass for the blessing of babies, and at home they make an altar that represents the Bethlehem manger where Jesús was born. They pray and sing to the niños dioses, and then distribute sweets, sparklers, and mini candles. In some houses they break piñatas.

I never went to a retreat, but my father-in-law took my husband to a retreat in the Casa Santa de Ejercicios, so he has told me in more detail how the retreats work. They enter on Saturdays and must buy a laminated badge that guarantees food and lodging in the Casa. Food is not of importance since they're there to sacrifice—it's just soup and beans. On Sundays they have a Mass and a procession to the Cruz del Perdón. They're allowed out only on Saturdays and Sundays and the rest of the time, it's total confinement. They must always carry their soga and disciplina. In the mornings, they have Mass

[33] A la entrada del Rancho Hotel Atotonilco el Viejo se encuentra la Cruz del Perdón, donde simbólicamente los Peregrinos domingo a domingo depositan una piedra que simboliza el desprendimiento de sus pecados. https://residencialatotonilc.wixsite.com/atotonilco-el-viejo/atotonilco

after breakfast, later prayer, then they continue with the flogging or flagellation. They walk after the one who carries the cross and each person is free to hit himself on his back—no one else can hit him—with the soga, the severity of the strikes in relation to his sins. What follows is another rest, then prayer, lunch, prayer, rest, and later dinner that ends with prayer. At week's end, the first-time attendees are crowned with thorns that they either bought in a puesto or made with mesquite thorns from the roads near Atotonilco.

On Saturdays or Sundays, the religious brothers gave permission to those doing the retreat to buy what they needed: candle, a crown, a veil, a soga with its disciplina, a Christ, and a bell. If they were attending for the first time, they had a godfather or padrino who had invited them, and he'd give them what they needed. On the last day of confinement in the Casa Santa de Ejercicios, they do a farewell mass where they dress in white, wear a crown, a veil, and light a candle; in reality, the meaning of the candle is not clear, some say that it's in gratitude, others that it's like a request, and others that it's an offering.

Mass concludes the spiritual exercises. A nun gives communion to the penitents who wear white, have on a veil, and hold a candle that has been used but is now extinguished. Women can attend the retreats as well, but they must do so with other women since it's not permitted to have women and men together. Some take children with them, and for them, there are small disciplinas.

Selling those items—and more—kept us busy. If we didn't have what a buyer was looking for, we had radios that we used to ask my godparents if they had them in their store or in their cellar. Or if the buyer was going to make a wholesale purchase, we'd send him to the store my godparents have in their home. I sold so much that I had to do an inventory where I balanced out what had been sold, counted the money, and moved some items to my godparents, and told them what new things to bring, and sent them the money. In the afternoon, I gave them more money, a lot of money.

My godparents had a lot of confidence in me, didn't have to check on me, and if something broke, they did not charge me or scold me. In those days, the food stalls were in front of the church and if I had a craving for a drink like *agua fresca* or fruit or anything else, I had permission from my godparents to buy whatever I liked.

Sundays were busy days. We moved the puesto with a van that they called the chilera or a locker. The street that passes in front of the Temple was closed so that more stalls could be set up. My godparents' puesto covered the sidewalk and part of the street. At about 10:00 a.m. we took everything out of storage, put it in a truck, and set up the new puesto. About 6:00 or 7:00 p.m. we closed it and it took several of us to take it down. Yes, my godparents have a good business, and this allows them to live well. I was fortunate to work for them.

In my godmother's shop—different from the puesto—she sold wholesale to the religious brothers and to Atotonilco merchants and others. On Sundays, she went to the stalls to collect money. Or to see if someone had items to sell at a good price, such as a cheerful and kind woman from Mexico City who sold medals. Or an American who sold items and always gave me something, like a Virgin of Guadalupe that I still have. The biggest sales were when a club came from La Barca, also known as Santa Mónica de la Barca from Jalisco—they came to stay at the Casa de Ejercicios, but they also took advantage of the time to shop. There was little rest for us in the puesto during those times. Sometimes people came who spoke Spanish, but some spoke other languages such as Nahuatl, and I loved it because they wore the typical costumes of our ancestors and retained their mother tongue, braids, petticoats, the colorful costumes with voluminous fabrics.

~

Apoyo para Gente Emprendedora—called Apoyo—headed by Ezequiel Mojica, helps people either start their own businesses or strengthen existing ones, all in low-income neighborhoods in San Miguel and in rural communities such as Los Ricos where women use the loans to support their fledgling efforts in Atotonilco.[34]

***The News* article by Dianne follows:** I accompany Ezequiel and his assistant on his next stop, a scheduled monthly meeting to visit with Apoyo's loan recipients in Los Ricos de Abajo.

When we arrive in this village of a couple hundred people, the only sound comes from a distant radio. It's noon and from the San Miguel radio station, we hear Pedro Vargas singing "Ave María," a village version of the twelve o'clock whistle. Eerie, otherworldly, with the music bouncing from the stucco walls.

I follow Ezequiel up a rocky path, concentrating on every step lest we slip backwards, to a house with concrete floors and walls, topped by a metal roof. Greeting us are our seventy-three-year-old hostess, Piedad, and her fellow grantees, María, Virginia, and Irma.

---

[34] Adapted from an article in The News, Mexico City, 2008. Dianne Walta Hart. Early on Los Ricos was identified as a community with severe economic need. The villagers took advantage of opportunities for growth and improvement through Apoyo's loan program. When FTH and the English Program with tutoring and scholarships came to Los Ricos, the parents saw the value and were ready . It has been a good fit indeed.

Piedad welcomes us into her house. She has such a big smile that it looks as if it comes from a lifetime of exuberance. My guess is that while her apron goes on the first thing in the morning and doesn't come off until late at night, the smile stays.

Inside are what looks like a love seat and chair—a plaid blanket covers the longer seat, and a red and white sheet is spread over the shorter one—both perched on four bricks precariously placed under each corner. It takes me a minute before I realize that they're old car seats, one from the back of a car and the other from the front. Recycling at its best.

The women hand over their payments, demonstrating what Ezequiel had earlier told me: in Los Ricos, they always pay back their loans. A donor has established a revolving fund within Apoyo just for that village; the grantees know that if they don't pay back the money, others cannot receive a loan nor can they, as first grantees, apply for a second one. The women—and they are all women because no men showed up for the original meeting—are all related and, according to Ezequiel, more conscientious and religious than people in San Miguel where repayment records are not as good.

I start asking them about their lives. Ezequiel had warned us earlier that people from Mexico's villages rarely open up to strangers. He's of Otomí ancestry, one of them, and I clearly am not. I try to make my case by telling them about my connection with their community. As good luck would have it, months earlier I had interviewed one of the women, Irma,[35] and I had given her two copies of the newspaper article about her. So even though I am acquainted with only one, the rest know the organizations—Feed the Hungry and the English program—I'm connected with.

I ask them questions, drawing on my own interest and curiosity. When they answer, they usually find something funny to say. For example, how many have TV sets? Three do. When the fourth says, "I did," then pauses and adds, "but it's broken," everyone laughs. When I ask who has a car, they think the idea of that is pretty funny, but they really crack up when one says that she has a female donkey and Piedad says she has two wheelbarrows. The momentum continues with their responses to cell phones: no one has one, but Irma had earlier owned one and, with the rhythm of a comic, she adds that it fell in the water.

On the weekends, they walk for the hour to Atotonilco where, with the

---

[35] Irma is the mother of Fernando Bárcenas, one of the university graduates from Naciones Unidas. Another son, Agustín, migrated to the United States during junior high school, was an honors graduate from a New York City high school, and is presently in the U. S. Army.

help of Apoyo-financed businesses, they sell food or water to pilgrims and tourists. Some of the women are considering expanding their efforts by marketing religious objects like rosaries, crowns of thorns, and the self-flagellation whips favored by some of the faithful at the Santuario de Atotonilco.

For the moment, though, Piedad sells chicken soup and roast beef. With her first loan, she bought a gas grill and a gas tank; she successfully paid that back, applied for a second, and with that, she bought her wheelbarrows. Irma sells the same food as Piedad. María sells gorditas (little fat tortillas that are split in half to hold a filling); before her loan she cooked over wood, now with gas. Virginia sells water in glass bottles, whereas before they were plastic and blew over when a wind came along.

With the Apoyo loans and advice from Ezequiel, they've rented a place in Atotonilco to store their supplies rather than dragging everything back and forth on the dusty and rocky road. The economy of Los Ricos is based on bartering; they grow most of what they eat, but still have to interact with the peso economy for cooking oil, chilies, and other expenses. That's where the profits come in. This is their only way to obtain currency.

Ezequiel tries to see if there is something else that would help them to succeed in their businesses. With the timing that had been so obvious an hour earlier in the classroom, he adds, "Well, other than money." Barrels of laughter.

"Improvement in transportation?" he asks. "For example, how about a bus to San Miguel or to Atotonilco?" Well, maybe, but they rarely go to San Miguel and when they do, it's not on a schedule, and as the discussion goes on, it turns out that they're accustomed to the long Atotonilco walk. They see no reason to change.

The women, three of whom are widows, say their lives in the village are peaceful. An elected official, a community delegado, resolves problems, when necessary, but usually the women are safe—no robberies, no burglaries, no knives, and they can make the walk between Atotonilco and Los Ricos without being concerned for their safety, even at night. I asked about the packs of wild dogs I'd heard about. They all agreed *that* was trouble.

Then out of nowhere comes a cooler that the Apoyo loan had allowed María to buy. Inside are her gorditas for us stuffed with nopales and red peppers. The women hadn't known Ezequiel would come accompanied by someone other than his aide. I notice that they make sure we eat before they do.

After we've eaten, Ezequiel reminds the women he'll be back. He doesn't say it, but I know that even if his car doesn't start, even if his friend can't drive him, and even if the Coca Cola truck doesn't give him a ride, he'll go with the bus to the highway drop-off spot, then walk an hour, and be in Los Ricos on the first Wednesday of the month at noon, just in time to hear Pedro Vargas sing "Ave María" on someone's radio and meet up with the women entrepreneurs.

ACKNOWLEDGEMENTS

Carolyn and Dianne, Los Ricos de Abajo, 2012

Without Michael Chadwick's vision, none of this would have happened, and he continues to support the scholarships. He will forever receive our gratitude. The English teachers and their friends contribute and solicit additional funds. We also thank the people who simply invited the teachers to dinner parties and found themselves contributing to not only the scholarships, but also to the comedor, flush toilets, and bodega. (You know who you are.) We additionally thank the board of Feed the Hungry San Miguel for their generosity.

Credit for managing our finances and the scholarships goes to Chris Peeters at Feed the Hungry, Doug Lord, Bob Bowers, and Lucha Jiménez Rodríguez.

Dianne Walta Hart accepts all responsibility for the students' translations. Geoff and Guillermina Hargreaves helped develop many of the questions the students were asked, assisted with idiomatic translations, and translated Yessenia's poetry. Thank you to Tom Hart and Marie Hart Mattison for reading the manuscript, finding all sorts of errors, and making wonderful suggestions.

Credit also goes to all the students, Lucha, and volunteer teachers for contributing (for years!) to this manuscript. Thank you to Judyth Hill and Mary Meade of Wild Rising Press.

One hundred percent of every contribution goes to our scholarship fund, as do the profits from this book. For more information on how to donate, see www.feedthehungrysma.org and be sure to add a note that your donation is for the Los Ricos scholarships.

~

You don't really see the world if you look through only your own window.
—UKRAINIAN PROVERB

Sí, ya somos abuelitas de nuestros alumnos.
—LUCHA

Made in United States
North Haven, CT
12 December 2023

45555374R00104